The Novels of Graham Greene

The Novels of Graham Greene

A Thematic Study in the Impact of Childhood on Adult Life

P.N. Pandit

PRESTIGE

Published by
Prestige Books
3/28, East Patel Nagar, New Delhi 110 008
in association with
Indian Society for Commonwealth Studies
New Delhi

Price: [illegible]
1989
ISBN 81-85218-17-X

Jacket design by
3-A Corporation,
New Delhi 110 002

Phototypesetting by
data culture
New Delhi 110 065
Ph. 6431070

Printed by
Mehra Offset Press
New Delhi 110 002

Contents

Introduction

> *For the writers it is always said that the first twenty years of life contain the whole experience— the rest is observation, but I think it is equally true of all of us.*[1]

The above statement, made by Brown, a character in Graham Greene's novel, *The Comedians*, is a striking piece of self-revelation on the part of the author. This year, in 1989, Greene completes eighty-five years of life. Of these, the first twenty or so contain all the experiences that are basic or formative in his life. The rest of his life, containing almost six decades of literary output, show nothing new, only the same recurrent patterns or themes, the same discussions well-established in early life. His first successful novel, *The Man Within* came out in 1929, and in 1985, *The Tenth Man* was in the book-market. To use a metaphor, his creative output spanning more than sixty years, forms an E.E.G (Electro encephalogram) of his major concerns or themes. His childhood is the brain-centre from which the lines begin and are traced through his life-graph. These lines are quite uniform and show little undulation since the same brain waves move regularly outward. If my metaphor is not far-fetched, my idea must be clear. Greene's characters relive his own dreams and frustrations. In so many different thin disguises, his characters show the ineradicable stamp of his childhood experiences. Therefore, it may be said, the key to understanding Greene as a writer, is his childhood. Greene himself subscribes to the theory that childhood and adolescence form a blue-print. Later life is built faithfully on this design. Modern research in genetics upto the discoveries of the Nobel prize winner, Hargovind Khorana, has proved the influential role of heredity in a man's life. The basic blueprint of a man's character or personality is contained in the genes, the basic building blocks of the body. The building blocks of Greene's characters exist in their childhood consciousness—their store-house of early memories. Here childhood means, the period of the earliest sensible reactions to life when the mental processes begin formation of concepts.

There is already a plethora of criticism on Greene's religious and secular views. The hottest disputes about him rage regarding the religion he portrays or conforms to in his works. Is he a Catholic novelist or merely a novelist who happens to be a Catholic convert? Some critics trace his secular or political ideology to Leftism. Many have noted the influence of Conrad and James on his works. And yet others see the existentialist bent of his vision, comparing him to Kafka and Dostoevsky and nineteenth century Decadents. In the whole gamut of critical work on him, nowhere is found a comprehensive work on the influence of childhood on his works, although there are numerous casual references to this aspect of his novels. It is therefore important to highlight the importance of studying childhood (Greene's own and that of many characters in his novels) to see the full significance of the themes in his novels and to understand fully the characters he creates. In fact, Greene's childhood helps to explain his religious and secular ideologies in a clearer light.

Greene writes everything to project the great world of his childhood. In his attitude, he is being loyal to his earliest impressions. Greene's views are very similar to Bernanos' expressed in "Les Enfants Humilies":

> .... I do know why I write. I write to justify myself. In whose eyes? .... In the eyes of the child I was. Whether that child speaks to me any longer or not, I shall never acknowledge his silence; I shall keep on answering him.[2]

Greene seems to always hear the child in him speaking to him and his works are his answers to the child's eternal questions. They explain his miseries and sorrows. Carolyn D. Scott notes the same fact:

> No critic can escape the childhood theme in Greene, for it is the one obsession out of which his tragedies grow.

Graham Greene's childhood was actually "The Lost Boyhood of Judas." His sense of utter futility regarding life, the stifling puritanical environment of his school at Berkhamstead, his alienation from his school mates, his tortures at the hands of bullies, his truancies to the commons and his desire to end his life by playing Russian roulette and taking poison—all these form a background to understanding his characters. These experiences form a symbiosis in Greene's childhood experience and the characters of his novels recreate the same in their childhood. Greene's principal (or main) characters are properly termed "anti-heroes," since unlike traditional heroes, they are disintegrated personalities, sometimes neurotic and sometimes criminal. They are victims of their childhood memories. They stumble through life, continually reverting to days in childhood where the causes of their failure lie. A note of caution may be struck here. A one-to-one correspondence between Greene's early life and his characters is unwise. The characters do not represent Greene as he is to-day but as he imagines people become who have had experiences similar to his. Thus, the killers Pinkie and Raven only embody Greene's murderous instincts as a revenge on one's miserable plight in childhood. Greene is similarly fictionalizing early experiences by creating Andrews and Anthony Farrant, Conder and Minty who suffer from father hatred and school phobia, and characters like the Lieutenant and Doctor Jowett who brood over the shortcomings and humiliations of early life. These anti-heroes are Judas figures who betray Christ or the idea of Infinite goodness because their childhoods were "lost."

Greene underwent a psychoanalysis at the age of sixteen. He was greatly benefited by it for a time. This was also the beginning of his interest in child-psychology and psycho-analysis. His art of character-portrayal shows the strong influence of psycho-analytical techniques. His characters continually reflect on their past, trying to trace their present neurosis to childhood traumas. There is an extensive use of dreams to interpret hidden subconscious desires. Many interior monologues are presented in stream-of-consciousness. Modern research proves the power of human memory to "tyrannize" man, to control his behaviour. Scientific research of memory mechanisms proves that the past can hold all the keys to our present behaviour. Modern psychoanalytical schools like the Transactional School make use of the findings of Sigmund Freud to help people to regain mental health by specific techniques. These techniques take into account the presence of three ego states in man—the Parent, the Child and the Adult. These ego states are subconscious recordings of man's transactions with parents and society and of personal reactions to the world in early life. These recordings or memories may "replay" in later life influencing reactions to events and experiences.

In Greene's childhood, something went wrong in his education that was to develop a sexual conflict in him. The puritanism of his school warped the sexual instinct. We may see from his works clearly that his mind was trained to inhibition for his characters have an unnatural sexual life. They either find sex revolting like Pinkie or the human body repulsive like Minty. Sex is painful coition to them. In many the sexual impulse warps the sense of guilt and frustrates their desire to find a full healthy sexual life. Greene experienced frustration in his first love affair when he was seventeen. Most of the love-affairs in his novels fail owing to lack of mutual trust, to rivalry or some type of guilt.

A great paradox about Greene is the fact that though he is one of England's most successful writers, he has always been suffering from a failure-fixation since childhood. The word "Fixation" denotes that his aspirations gravitate towards failure. This very love for failure or natural attraction to failure is the chief trait of his characters. Failure is destined in most of the ventures and schemes described in his novels. The origin of this failure-fixation is difficult to pinpoint, but it certainly has its genesis in Greene's childhood. First, he realized intuitively that failure was inherent in all human enterprises. This sense of failure was reinforced when his first attempts at writing met with no success. Even now, the same doom seems to hover over all his successes. Some of his characters like Krogh in *England Made Me* and Doctor Jowett in *The Great Jowett* are successes in the worldly sense of money and fame, but an impending sense of defeat hovers over them. Greene does not despise his failed characters. He loves them. As he says even God loves failures. Greene believes he has had his share of failures in life. Are they really failures in the worldly sense? His success and renown as a novelist point the other way. Is it then just a sense of failure, a view that things are failures in a more spiritual sense that haunts him since childhood? He writes:

> If there are recurrent themes in my novels it is perhaps only because there have been recurrent themes in my life. Failure seemed then to be one of them.[4]

At Berkhamstead, at his home, a green baize door separated the family quarters from the school dormitories. This door becomes a symbol of the divide between two worlds, or two realities co-existing in antithesis. As Greene writes in the Prologue to *Lawless Roads:*

> One began to believe in Heaven because one believed in Hell.

While this side of the baize door which contained the family quarters signified innocence, the other side containing the dormitories with wicked children denoted experience. This duality of human nature which was suggested by the partition of home from dormitory and which gave a concrete shape to his intuitions forms the basis of the sense of dichotomy in his religious and secular views as expressed in his writings. In fact, when we realize that Greene's awareness came from childhood instincts, we begin to see clearly the logic and reason in his pronouncements on religion. Those who seek an explanation of his paradoxes in his conversion to Catholicism, fail to understand him. Many people trained to look for a cosy, conventional approach to religion are baffled by his views. Greene, for instance, makes the sinner beloved of God and deserving more than others of divine grace. Adulterers and criminals are God's favourite candidates for salvation. To right-minded Catholics and Christians, Greene's stance is shocking. But when we study the childhood experiences that moulded his views—his awareness of duality—we begin to see that there are no anomalies in his views. We realize that at another level, Greene is fighting against dogma and establishing the heart of the matter.

Throughout his works, opposing, contradictory creeds and ideologies are counterpointed. Thus Communism and Catholicism confront each other in *The Lawless Roads*. Idealism vies with cynicism, materialism with faith. Other characters, representing different, antithetical beliefs are brought into collision. And in the end, Greene brings about a reconciliation between the opposites by showing that they contain complementary traits. The one reflects the other in some subtle way. In short, opposing creeds lie on either side of the baize door of his childhood.

Many Greene characters like Andrews in *The Man Within* have dual or multiple personalities. They are subject to frequent waverings of emotion, being pulled in opposite directions by God and Satan. Greene realized early in life that man could have a multiple nature. He himself was a manic-depressive—his mood alternating between dejection and high spirits.

The sense of Evil hangs heavily on Greene's mind. Early in life, Greene saw at school, characters like Crandon and Collifax and the bully, Carter who had the genuine quality of evil in them. They all basked in a hell that later took the shape of the terrible vista called Greeneland, where evil walks in triumph. A reinforcement of this view came from Greene's early reading. The character that supplied him with a prototype once and for all was Visconti Mastino della Scala, in *The Viper of Milan*. Greene's novels are filled with evil characters like Pinkie, Raven, Yusef and Harry Lime.

Greene's depiction of places in his novels are projections of that hell he saw as a child. He is a master painter of dark, ominous colours. His landscapes are one long stretch of crime and corruption. In fact, his descriptions rival those of Dante's "Divine Inferno" and like Dante, Greene portrays places like different circles of hell where injustice and war prevail. As a child, Greene was inclined to the morbid aspects of life. The general squalor and seediness of his school-building left a deep impact on him and conditioned his reactions to the world. Seediness and squalor characterize places like West Africa and Mexico in his books. We know from Greene's autobiography that as a child he suffered from a fear of fire, drowning and witches and the pains of illness and a dental extraction left him very sensitive to pain in general. These experiences influenced his literary sensibilities and the settings of his novels emanate from his store-house of early fears. We may attribute to Greene what he himself says about Pinkie, the juvenile criminal in *Brighton Rock:*

> A brain was capable only of what it could conceive, and it couldn't conceive what it had never experienced. . . .[5]

There are two aspects of innocence that Greene is generally concerned with in his novels. First, innocence in children is easily vulnerable to the corruption of adults. Corruption is so prevalent all around children that many of them soon succumb to it and they suddenly lose the bliss of the simplicity and ignorance of childhood. Many Greene child-characters like Brigitta, Anna Hilfe, Coral, Else and the gang-leader in the short story "The Destructors" have graduated too early from childhood to adult knowledge. "The spot of decay" in them has fully blighted their childhood. The children with their forbidden knowledge are recreations of the smarmy youths in Greene's home-town to whom "sexual experience came too early." Sex is, in fact, the main type of corruption children are susceptible to. A wide gap exists in the vision of life that children have and that adults have. Greene brings this idea out in some short stories like "The Innocent." Unfortunately this innocence of vision is stained by the intrusion of corrupt adults into the world of children. Children must keep away from the goings-on of adults.

This is the moral of Greene's children books in the transport series in which Greene plays a champion of the child's rights. Innocent children suffer in war and are sometimes victims of the money-hungry corrupt adults. In short, if children must not grow up to a crippled life later on, childhood innocence must be preserved. There is yet another aspect of this theme Greene touches upon in some novels. People who grow up without maturing in their vision are dangerous to themselves and to others. Here 'maturing' does not mean the power to indulge in corruption..It means to be able to cope with the goings-on in the world of adult reality. The unformed mind attracts evil people to exploit it or it might so turn out, that the immature person has an idealism that proves ruthless and harmful as in the case of Alden Pyle in *The Quiet American.*

Greene's vision of reality may be compared to that of his contemporaries—Auden and Orwell— and to that of some others like Sartre, Dickens and Kipling. All these writers suffered in childhood for various reasons like family troubles, financial vicissitudes or unhappy school experiences. Their reactions to these early experiences were not all the same, however. While writers like Kipling, Munro, Sartre, Orwell, Auden and Greene himself reacted by a sense of revenge, bitter hatred or sense of justice outraged, Dickens' reactions were positive. His early sufferings made him sympathetic and compassionate to the outcaste and downtrodden in society. Greene, Henry James and Sartre became aware of the presence of Evil and the inevitability of death in the world when they were children. They all portray themes related to these aspects in their novels. We also note the influence of early reading which has been profound both on Greene and Sartre.

The implications of the loss of childhood are grave. Greene extends the meaning of the term 'childhood' to include that state of pristine innocence from which mankind and modern civilisation has evolved. According to Greene, Africa still retains to some extent, memories of the childhood or genesis of mankind. Untouched and unspoiled by the contraptions and harmful sophistication of civilisation as we know it in Europe, Africa is the birthplace of man. Greene says that a subconscious desire in man prompts him to return to that state of spontaneous, blissful existence that Africa denotes. That is why early European explorers like Mungo Park and now Greene himself undertook the dangerous trek into the heart of the Dark Continent. They were actualizing a spiritual necessity. In *Journey without Maps*. Greene describes the feelings of having come home as he trekked through Liberia. Here he regained his love of living, killed by the spiritual vacuity of western civilisation. The sense of pleasure is keener in Africa like the instinctive delight of a child to nature. William Wordsworth, in his "Ode to Childhood," lamented the loss of this same childhood vision. In Greene's novel, *A Burnt-Out Case,* Querry takes a trip to West Africa and seems to stumble on Pendele—a word signifying a natural state of existence in which singing and dancing take place spontaneously and one regresses to a state of feeling and no thoughts. Querry's peace is, however, shattered, as civilisation catches up with him in the form of a journalist who wants to give him publicity. In his novel in a comic vein, *Travels with my Aunt,* Greene takes Pulling back to a state of childhood pleasures through picaresque adventures. He regains the excitement of living which was dulled by the routine formalities of a bank clerk's life. Greene's theory is that man must retain his childhood consciousness of joy in lifc, if hc is to enjoy himself even when he grows up. Civilisation is at an adult stage today. The great mistake it has made is that it has not preserved the innocent codes of living . This means he has exchanged too much materialism for the qualities of the heart.

The implications of Greene's ideas are that mankind is responsible today more than ever for safeguarding the innocence and happiness of its children all over the world.

We need to take a long view or journey backwards like Greene recommends and we shall find that a symmetry informs all the different aspects of Greene's vision of childhood. Like a child's map which takes shape gradually, all the different themes discussed in this book take on a co-ordinated meaning. To understand Greene, one must, like T.S. Eliot, arrive at the place where one began and know the place for the first time. The journey Greene began at his birthplace Berkhamstead takes a circuitous route that will end in

Berkhamstead, in his childhood, that is in childhood memories. Meanwhile, Greene goes on writing. Themes keep emerging from the chambers of childhood consciousness. The recurrent patterns are there always. We may attribute to Greene the words of Francois Mauriac:

> Even if he withdraws and shuts his eyes, his most distant past will begin to ferment. His childhood and youth is enough to provide a born novelist with an immense amount of literary nourishment. Nobody can stop the flow of the river which flows from him.[6]

NOTES

1. Greene, Graham, *The Comedians,* The Bodley Head, London 1966, p. 74.
2. Bernanos, "Les Enfants Humilies," as quoted in Kenneth Allott and Miriam Farris, *The Art of Graham Greene,* Hamish Hamilton, London, 1951, p. 25.
3. D. Scott, Carolyn, "The Witch at the Corner" in *Graham Greene: Some Critical Considerations,* Univ. of Kentucky Press, Lexington, 1967, p. 7.
4. Greene, Graham, *A Sort of Life,* Penguin, London, 1971, p. 154.
5. Greene, Graham, *Brighton Rock,* Heinemann, London 1955, p. 306.
6. Mauriac, Francois, "God and Mammon" in Miriam Allott's *Novelists on the Novel,* Routledge, Kegan Paul, London, 1959, p. 108.

The Lost Boyhood of Judas

In ancient shadows and twilights
Where childhood had strayed
The world's great sorrows were born
And its heroes were made
In the lost boyhood of Judas
Christ was betrayed.[1]

It is noteworthy that Graham Greene was greatly impressed by the lines quoted above and they seem to form a refrain in his works—particularly with reference to his major characters. The novelist was tempted to quote the last two lines in his short story, "The Basement Room." They are taken from A.E's poem "Germinal."

Christ is Goodness Incarnate, an embodiment of God's word: and his betrayal by Judas is a prototype of mankind's betrayal of God's infinite love for him. Man sins and wallows in the lust of flesh and trespasses all God's commandments with impunity. But the purport of the poem is that Judas, one of Christ's twelve disciples, who betrayed Jesus for a handful of silver, was not completely responsible for his act. His will and intellect were influenced by primal forces of evil and sin deep down in his being, his psyche. These forces can be traced back to the pristine childhood of man, generations ago, when in the Garden of Eden, Adam and Eve committed the original sin of eating the forbidden fruit. An interpretation of the symbolism of the biblical story leads us to believe that man sinned by over-riding God's laws and thereby doomed posterity to suffering. This early state of abandonment from divine love and grace is the "lost childhood" of man, of Judas of history and of all the Judas-like characters that move through Greene's literary creations. It is to this primal source of life, to childhood we must go to find the roots of the psychic deviations that mar and wreck the lives of Greene's heroes. Maria Montessori, a world-renowned educationist, whose Montessori system of education is popular all over the world, throws light on this great phenomenon of the loss of innocence:

> From earliest antiquity it has been recognised that there are two natures, in man—man as he was created and man as fallen, the fall being attributed to an original sin. It has been recognised that this sin in itself is trivial, out of all proportion to the immensity of its consequences, but implying a forsaking of the creative spirit, of the laws laid down in creation. After it, man becomes like a drifting ship, driven by chance, with no defence against the obstacles of his environment or against the illusions of his mind. Hence he is lost. This conception. a synthesis of the philosophy of life, finds a singular and illuminating counterpart in the life of the child. A very trivial thing leads to deviation, something hidden and tenuous that creeps in under the guise of love and help, but which at bottom comes from a blindness in the adult soul, a veiled and unconscious egotism, that is really a diabolical power working against the child.[2]

The loss of innocence may be occasioned by "a veiled egotism," "a blindness" on the part of the adult whose love and help is forced on to the growing plant at the wrong time and may like excess of bad manure, stunt its growth. We notice this in the form of parental interference.

The concept of the loss of innocence, "the idea that the cruelties and betrayals of adult lives are born in childhood,"[3] may be termed 'Judas Complex.' This term is first ascribed to Greene's characters in the *Times Literary Supplement* of the 17th Sept. 1971. The use of "Complex" in the term gives it a psychological overtone suggestive of terms like Oedipus, Electra, inferiority and superiority complex. The term "complex" in psychology denotes a knot of ideas embedded in the subconscious which causes an obstruction to the normal flow of consciousness and influences behaviour patterns in man.

Throughout his works, Greene recurrently maintains that experiences in early life leave an ineradicable stamp on the formation of a man's character. There is no modification possible with the help of later education or indoctrination. Not all psychologists would subscribe to his view on the irreversibility of effects, but it reveals Greene's own thinking in his novels. What most psychologists do confirm is the fact that the first few years are the time when the blueprint of man's life are etched out. According to L.S. Kubie, a psychiatrist:

> It is possible to make one certain deduction: namely that early in life, a central emotional position is frequently established. . . . The clinical fact which is already evident is that once a central emotional position is established early in life, it becomes the affective position to which that individual will tend to return automatically for the rest of his life. This in turn may constitute either the major safeguard or the major vulnerability of his life.[4]

One may intend to deal with Greene's theory of childhood, at two levels as revealed in his works. At the first, the influence of certain events in his own childhood on his attitudes in later life. And at the other level, the shaping influences of the childhood experiences of his major characters on their lives.

In fact, most of Greene's characters have strong autobiographical element in them. They may not completely represent Greene as he is now, but represent his experiences as a child. Greene's characters invariably follow a set pattern in their lives. They experience a particular syndrome of emotions, namely, boredom and sense of futility, alienation from their milieu and injustice, rebellion and flight, revenge, sex, guilt and frustration, despair and failure, manic—depressive neurosis, wish for death often culminating in suicide.

First, we must read a brief life-sketch of Greene up to his adolescence, somewhere upto the age of twenty-one. Then we shall be able to draw parallels with his characters. In fact, his experiences constitute the key to unlock the psychology of his heroes.

The sources for information of Greene's childhood are:

(a) His autobiographical books: *A Sort of Life* and *Ways of Escape*, written over a gap of ten years. The first came out in 1971 and the second in 1980.
(b) His travelogues: *The Journey Without Maps* (1936) and *The Lawless Roads* (1939).
(c) His essays: "The Last Word," which was a contribution to an anthology entitled, *The Old School*, edited by Greene himself in 1934 and "The Lost Childhood" (1951).
(d) Some poetry collected in an anthology entitled, *Babbling April* (1925).
(e) An autobiographical fragment called "The Revenge" (1963).

From the above mentioned works, one may draw evidence for Greene's childhood experiences in the sequence—boredom and meaninglessness, alienation and injustice, truancies from school, experience of undergoing psychoanalysis, recurrence of boredom, death wish and attempts at suicide.

Graham Greene was born in 1904, in Berkhamstead, England, very near the "pain—threshold," a term coined by William James in his book, *The Varieties of Religious Experience*. He was educated at Berkhamstead School of which his father was headmaster. Graham was a sensitive boy and felt stifled in the conventional, middle-class, Anglican Protestant environment of his school. He had an imagination far advanced than that of his school fellows and was attacked by a sense of ennui and boredom by all that life offered him. The school rules inhibiting exercise of free thinking, enforcing doctrines of morality and the general filth festering under the surface of the prudery in sex, alienated him from his class-fellows and his whole school. For the first thirteen years, he was haunted with boredom and a sense of utter meaninglessness in existence. They add to his boredom, there was the betrayal and alienation by his friends. He was branded as a member of the Quisling's party, represented by his father, and humiliated in a game that was played in those days. He had to stand with back turned, counting ten, while the other boys advanced to touch his back. This humiliation left a permanent scar on his mind and the experience reappears in the creation of the character called Andrews in *The Man Within.* Greene also had tormentors who bullied him. Carter and Watson, his schoolmates, became, in his works, the prototypes of the injustice of the world. Greene recalls in *A Sort of Life:*

> For there was a boy at my school called Carter who perfected during my fourteenth and fifteenth years, a system of mental torture based on my difficult situation. Carter had an adult imagination—he could conceive the conflict of loyalties, loyalties to my age-group, loyalty to my father and brother. The sneering nicknames were inserted like splinters under the nails.[5]

Greene's hatred of his days at Berkhamsted is central to all his writing. *The Captain and the Enemy* (1988) opens with a reminder of those years—his position as 'a collaborator in occupied territory,' his suicidal boredom, his wish to escape like a character from Henty to Haggard to a just South American republic where he could pass his days capturing mule trains laden with gold.

However, Greene never seriously desired revenge on Carter. It was another boy called Watson who had switched loyalties from Greene to Carter. His betrayal had caused the greatest pain.

> Watson imitated him (Carter) only at a blundering, unimaginative level. Alone he would have had no power to hurt. Nonetheless, it was on Watson that I swore revenge, for with his defection my isolation had become almost complete.[6]

Greene's mind smouldered to avenge this torture. He met Watson again after many years in December 1951, in Kuala Lumpur. Watson introduced himself but his memory seemed to differ with Greene's, for his voice and manner betrayed nothing of the strained relations they had had at school. From Watson he also found that Carter had died. Greene reflects in his autobiography:

> I wondered all the way to my hotel if I would ever have written a book had it not been for Watson and the dead Carter, if those years of humiliation had not given me an excessive desire to prove that I was good at something.[7]

Humiliation provokes one to excel one's rivals. Revenge and chase recur as a theme in Greene's works. Greene quotes Gaugin approvingly: "Life being what it is, one dreams of revenge."

When Graham Greene was seven years of age, he answered a questionnaire for his school House Gazette. As an answer to the question, "What is your favourite quotation?" he wrote, "I with two more to help me will hold the foe in play." Greene recalls in his autobiography:

> This reply surprises me for I remember liking better Aytoun's "The Execution of Montrose," which combined heroism and injustice. A child learns about injustice early.[8]

The theme of revenge always impressed Greene as a boy. He had read Q's *Foe Farrell* thrice or four times because it was a story of pursuit and revenge. At one dramatic moment in this story, Greene must have been thrilled, when the pursuer and pursued find themselves alone in an open boat in the Pacific. It was just the ideal situation in which Greene could identify himself with the avenger. Carter, who bullied him in school becomes in Greene's works the prototype of the tormentor. Even Greene's choice of names seems to bear a resemblance to real experience. In his book, *The Bear Fell Free,* the character Farrell who wishes to fly across the Atlantic, is betrayed by an ex-war hero called Carter. In Greene's essay *The*

Lost Childhood, Carter, the bully of schooldays is taken for a reincarnation of the dreaded Manichaean Visconti of *The Viper of Milan*. Identifying in Visconti his memories of Carter, Greene says:

> I had watched him pass by many a time in his black Sunday suit smelling of mothballs. His name was Carter. He exercised terror from a distance like a snow-cloud over the young fields.[9]

In *Our Man in Havana,* there is a Carter whom Wormold decides to kill. This Carter is a counter-spy who killed Hasselbacher. That name, Carter, Greene's first tormenter, has established itself well in its victim's psyche.

Greene tells us in his autobiography that the endless boredom of school life and his alienation from his schoolmates led to continual truancies. Greene reminisces:

> I don't know how long these sporadic escapes went on. They turned at some point (I would guess when I was eleven) into a better organised—and a more prolonged truancy.... 'Runs' I enjoyed for then I could be alone in the solitude of the countryside and, at this period of my life, I loved the country. It was my natural escape-route. On the wide stretches of Berkhamstead Common, seamed with the abandoned trenches of the Inns of Court, O.T.C., among the gorse and heather, and in the Ashbridge beechwood beyond, I could dramatize my loneliness and feel I was one of John Buchan's heroes making his hidden way across the Scottish moors with every man's hand against him.[10]

In Greene's novels the theme of pursuit is treated in many ways. In *The End of the Affair,* Bendrix and Sarah are pursued by the Hound of Heaven, God. All their attempts to escape from His grace by retaining their sinfulness is nullified by mysterious interventions of the Divine-pursuer. Pinkie Brown of *Brighton Rock*, is the only one who seems to succeed in escaping from the divine power of redemption, in his flight towards final damnation through suicide. *A Gun for Sale* is a novel with two pursuits in it. First, the policeman, Mather pursues James Raven, the criminal who has forged money. Secondly, Raven turns into the hunter himself, apprising Cholmondey and through him Sir Marcus Stein, the owner of Midland Steel at Nottwich. In *The Confidential Agent*, D. goes to England to negotiate a coal deal on behalf of his government with certain British mine owners and is pursued by counter agents, led by an aristocrat called L. The first two sections of the novel have headings suggestive of flight and chase and are entitled "The Hunted" and "The Hunter." There is a hair-breadth escape for D in the end of this thriller. In *The Ministry of Fear*, Rowe unwittingly comes to possess a role of film sought by the Nazis and their Allies and is pursued by secret agents in England. Then, he himself becomes the hunter and turns the tables on his enemies. He succeeds in running to earth Willi Hilfe, the leader of the Nazi fifth column. Rollo Marins, a writer of Westerns, in *The Third Man*, pursues the murderer of his friend, Harry Lime in Vienna. He gradually finds out that the murder of Lime was faked and that Lime himself is a criminal engaged in the penicillin adulteration racket. He finally corners Lime and kills him in the underground sewerage at Vienna.

Greene's flight to the moors in schooldays was actually the physical expression of his flight from his own self, from the madness and aching mania of his boredom. The priest in *The Power and the Glory*, is doing just the same thing as he runs constantly away from the police (Red Shirts) through forests and mountains. In fact, he is fleeing his own mental sickness. William Rose Benet confirms this view:

> For the priest is anointed; he is not actually fleeing God as the poet was in Francis Thompson's 'Hound of Heaven,' he is fleeing his own fear, praying desperately to preserve his loyalty to the greatest thing he knows, with all mankind, as it seems to him, arrayed against him, and no rest for the sole of his foot.[11]

The sentence echoes Greene's own experience of his early truancy at school:

> ... I was one of John Buchan's heroes making his hidden way across the Scottish moors with every man's hand against him.[12]

Greene himself has played the hunted man in later life, trying to escape boredom by courting different difficult situations. His book, *Ways of Escape* which came out in 1980, when he was about 76 years of age, has a title suggestive of flight. The book contains reminiscences on the many different ways in the past when he tried to escape his own maddening fears and uncertainties. For example, he says, writing has always been for him a way of escaping boredom:

> I write to escape from boredom. I find it unpleasant not to write. I sometimes wonder how all those who do not write, compose or paint, can manage to escape the madness, the melancholia and the fear, inherent in the human situation.[13]

So conditioned was Greene by the boredom at school that even the freedom of the holidays failed him:

> It had always been a feature of childhood: it would set in on the second day of the school holidays. The first day was all happiness, and after the horrible confinement and publicity of school, seemed to consist of light, space and silence. But a prison conditions its inhabitants. I never wanted to return to it . . . but yet I was so conditioned that freedom bored me unutterably.[14]

In the West, emotionally disturbed people usually have recourse to the Couch, a humorous name for the psycho-analyst's chamber. In 1920, when Greene was 16 years old, his father was worried by his truancies and melancholic depression and sent Graham to a psychiatrist called Kenneth Richmond in London. Greene reflects about his days with Richmond:

> Richmond belonged to no dogmatic school of psycho-analysis, so far as I can make out now: he was nearer to Freud than Jung, but Adler probably contributed. . . . My life with him did me a world of good, but how much was due to the analysis and how much to the breakfasts in bed, the quiet of Kensington Gardens, the sudden independence of my life, I would not like to say, nor whether the analysis was deep enough. In any case as Freud wrote, 'much is won if we succeed in transforming hysterical misery into common unhappiness.[15]

But Greene's temporary period of relief was soon followed by regression or relapse. The after-effects of the psycho-analysis were like the hangover following hallucinations caused by strong drugs. He was wrung dry by the experience and relapsed into catatonia—a state of apathy in which he lost all aesthetic taste for life. This state may be compared to the mescalin experience which Colin Wilson says:

> . . . plunges the taker into a kind of dream world, a world of inaction, where one has no defence against one's latent fears and fantasies.[16]

For years he could take no interest in any visual thing. Anything that appeared beautiful to others, elicited no reaction from him. "I was fixed in my boredom."[3]

From this boredom which seemed to almost burst his brain, he tried to escape by strange suicidal attempts. He drank hypo or hay-fever lotion, ate a bunch of deadly nightshade and took twenty aspirins before jumping into a swimming-pool. He had read about the Russian officers who used to invent macabre hazards to escape boredom. One man would slip a charge into a revolver and turn the chambers at random, and his friend would put the revolver to his head and pull the trigger. The chance was six to one in favour of life. To discover the possibility of enjoying again the visible world by risking its total loss, Greene began his experiments with Russian roulette when he was 17, using his brother's revolver. He would put the muzzle of the revolver in his right ear and pull the trigger not knowing whether he would shoot himself. The experiment was repeated several times till it failed to excite him anymore. Finally it became as mundane as taking an aspirin. After the sixth and last attempt, he gave up this particular campaign against boredom.

It seems fate had totally determined to preserve Greene for further challenges with boredom. His fight against boredom in later life took a more terrifying and desperate turn. It involved enterprises of the gravest risk, so that it would give him the necessary stimulation to free him from his apathy:

> A kind of Russian roulette remained too a factor in my later life, so that without previous experience of Africa, I went on an absurd and reckless trek through Liberia; it was fear of boredom which took me to Tabasco during the religious persecution, to the lepresorie in the Congo, to the Kikuyu reserve during the Mau Mau insurrection, to the emergency in Malay and to the French war in Vietnam. There, in the last three regions of clandestine war, the fear of ambush served me just as effectively as the revolver from the corner cupboard in the life-long war against boredom.[17]

Greene's obsession with death may also be gleaned in a few short stories and some poetry written in adolescence. All are tinged with a nostalgia for death which is regarded as freedom from the madness of existence. His first anthology of poems, *Babbling April* contains a piece called "The Gamble" (which was later elaborated into a prose piece "The Revolver in the Cupboard"). It poetizes his experience with Russian roulette.

> Place the revolver to my head,
> And pull the trigger.

Will it be mist and death.
At the bend of this sunset road.
Or life reinforced by the propinquity of death?
Either is gain.
It is a gamble which I cannot lose.[18]

"Mist and death" is as much a gain as "life reinforced" by this macabre thrill. In the same anthology, we have a poem entitled "Apres Vous." He tells his girl-friend that should she leave this world, he would follow close on her steps. He is shy in new company and so she should act as "a heavenly ice-breaker" by preceding him. He advises her to tell Michael, the angel, not to let him talk of the superiority of Hell's constitution. There is a similar wry humour in other poems. "If you were Dead" states he would have rest. In "Death and Cosmetics," he says that Death gives one the chance to "snatch a brief handicap before decay."

Greene's obsession with death is also found in two short stories written as a young man. The first entitled "The Second Death" which he wrote in 1930, describes a man who recovers from death and then meets God. The second is entitled "Proof Positive," in which a man gives a speech to a psychic society on the subject of psychic animation of a corpse. His speech is incoherent and at the end he falls down dead. It is discovered that the body had been dead for some days, but the spirit had been animating it. This was the "proof positive." In "The End of the Party," a small boy called Francis Morton dies because he is shocked by the touch of his brother's hand in the dark while playing hide and seek. He had always been afraid of the dark and the shock killed him. The story ends with his brother, Peter, clutching Francis' fingers in puzzled grief.

> His brain, too young to realize the full paradox, yet wondered with an obscure self-pity why it was that the pulse of his brother's fear went on and on when Francis was now where he had always been told there was no more terror and no more darkness.[19]

Death is considered a desirable consummation in Greene's works. After death, there is no more terror and no more darkness.

This brief life-sketch of Graham Greene sets the pattern of the career of his anti-heroes. First there is a feeling of meaning lessness in existence occasioned by a suffering of injustice at the hands of childhood friends, parents and society. Then there is rebellion or flight from this miserable state of affairs. Followed by an episode of revenge against the tormentors. Finally, there is despair and longing for death. Greene's anti-heroes embrace death willingly as a freedom from their neurotic lives.

Greene's characters are called anti-heroes because they do not conform to the traditional notion of the hero who is an epitome of spiritual and psychic harmony. Greene's characters are lost people subject to unhealthy, morbid states of mind resulting from traumas in carly life. They continually revert to and reflect on experiences of school and early home life where tormentors and ugly scenes existed. Every failure, bitterness and negative trait of their characters is traced to those years. Like Hamlet, they suffer from thought-blocking which obstructs any positive move in life. That is why they are "anti-heroes." They reverse the positive idealism of conventional heroes. They are more in line with Dostoevsky's Raskolnikov, Conrad's Jim and Mann's Felix Krull.

The following protagonists from Greene's novels may now be studied in some detail:

1. Francis Andrews of *The Man Within*
2. Anthony Farrant of *England Made Me*
3. Minty of *England Made Me*
4. Krogh of *England Made Me*
5. Conrad Drover of *It's a Battlefield*
6. Benjamin Jowett of *The Great Jowett*

These six above belong to a common class. They all suffer from either traumatic memories of school or parental domination, or both. They were alienated from society and friends in childhood.

7. Pinkie Brown of *Brighton Rock*
8. Raven of *A Gun for Sale*

The two above are criminals. The wound of childhood has never healed in them.

9. James Wormold of *Our Man in Havana*
10. Arthur Rowe of *The Ministry of Fear*

These two above dwell in the memories of their childhood, brooding over the loss of innocence. The adult world of realities is too painful for them.

11. The Lieutenant in *The Power and the Glory*

He suffers from the disillusionment of childhood hopes in his religion which has been incapable of removing the suffering of children in his country.

Francis Andrews of *The Man Within* (1929) is carried along by the influence of a ruined innocence to final damnation. Innocence is lost in a confrontation with an adult world of corruption and violence represented by his father who was overbearing and a school in which he could not adjust. He blames his father for all his miseries. A sea dog of the old Elizabethan tradition, his father was a tyrant at home:

> His father to his crew was a hero, a king, a man of dash, initiative. Andrews knew the truth—that he was a bully who killed his wife and ruined his son.[20]

His father beat him up mercilessly in order to infuse courage into him and sent him to school to study subjects like Greek so that he might boast about his son. But Andrews hated his school (a Greene factor) and always longed to run away from it. He was quite a misfit at school and felt alienated by the others (The Greene syndrome is building up) and was humiliated in a game they played.

> There was a game he had played at school, where one boy stood with back turned, counting ten, while the other boys advanced to touch his back.[21]

This reminds us of Greene's humiliation as a member of the Quisling's party at school. Andrews' hidden patriphobia or father-hatred is illuminated by continual flashbacks in the novel. For instance:

> Once his father had visited him at school. Andrews was in the gravel playground. . . . His father was shy, embarrassed, conscious suddenly of his own coarse bulk . . . 'Happy?,' he asked. Andrews had the instinctive cruelty of a child. He remembered his father at home, domineering, brutal, a conscious master, not chary of his blows to either child or wife. 'Very,' he said. His voice filled with artificial pleasure and he pronounced his words with artificial neatness.[22]

Andrews grew up to join his father's gang of smugglers, now led by Carlyon after his father's death. He thought he would now get his freedom and peace but his hopes were belied. There was no hope of any change to a better life, of any peace, except death.

Even after the death of his father, Andrews was haunted by him. Everyone found Andrews falling short of his father's stature. They remarked that it was strange that such a mountain could bring forth such a cowardly mouse. This continual comparison generated an inferiority complex. His father, therefore, became a presence within him, always reminding him of his shortcomings. So obsessed was he by this, that he longed to overthrow his father's psychic domination. This could be accomplished, he concluded, by betraying his father's gang of smugglers to the Excisemen at Lewes. In this way he would show that he could counteract the stranglehold of his father over him. He tells the Assizes the reason for his betrayal:

> It was because I had a father whom I hated and he was always being put before me as a model. It made me mad. And I'm a coward. You all know that. . . . I was afraid of being hurt and I hated the sea and the noise and the danger, and unless I did something it would have gone on for always and always. And I wanted to show that I had the power to smash all their plans.[23]

In betraying Carlyon and the smugglers, Andrews becomes bitterly conscious of a Judas-like guilt. Hadn't he committed the betrayal like Judas who had betrayed the father-figure Christ?

Since childhood he had been marked for alienation from his group. He remembered always the humiliating game played at school. The more he is isolated from the solidarity of the group of smugglers the world too forsakes him. At Lewes, he is called "a sneak thief," a damned informer" who was not fit to be among righteous people. In the court, he was afraid to look at the gallery because, there would be young, desirable women there who would watch him with contempt.

> The informer, traitor, Judas—not even honour among thieves.[24]

Carlyon's vengeance has been provoked and Andrews is in full flight from him. This is the rebellion and pursuit theme of the Greene syndrome. Andrews' utter weariness from pursuit is described in *The Man Within:*

> A sense of desolation passed over him, a wonder whether he would ever know peace from pursuit, and he gave an unconscious whimper like a rabbit snared.[25]

Elizabeth, whom he loved for the influence of pure sanctity she had on him, dies tortured by the smugglers for having given Andrews shelter. She had killed herself with the very knife he had left behind for his protection. Andrews considers her death as the logical death of his father's presence in him. All the failures of his life were traceable to his father's ill-treatment of him as a child. His father had made him a coward, and, therefore, he had not been able to muster up courage to defend Elizabeth. His self-awareness comes painfully:

> There had been no struggle with Carlyon, but only with his father. His father had made him a betrayer and his father had slain Elizabeth and his father was dead and out of reach. Out of reach. But was he? His father's was not a roaming spirit. It had housed itself in the son he had created. I am my father, he thought, and I have killed her.[26]

There is a miserable logic in this. His father was the instrument of all his life's failures. On Elizabeth's death, Andrews feels that his father in him, his cowardice and lust are exterminated.

> To his own surprise he felt happy and at peace for his father was slain and yet a self remained, a self which knew only peace and curiosity for the dark which deepened around him. . . . His father's had been a stubborn ghost, but it was laid at last.[27]

At the end of the Greene syndrome is death—the desirable end. The death of Elizabeth only aggravates Andrews' desire to follow her into the next world. A kind of terror of passing endless years in loneliness before he enters a blank eternity, overcomes him. He kills himself considering it an atonement for the weakness of the flesh which held the spirit in thrall. Death for him was a consummation of supreme importance just like it had always been for his creator, Greene.

Anthony Farrant of *England Made Me* is like Andrews, a result of soured father-son relationship in life. But while Andrews was mercilessly beaten up and subordinated by his father, Anthony was a victim of his father's "love." His father wanted his welfare, and wanted to mould him to his own specifications. But Anthony could not understand his father's love. His father was an honourable man who had a profound trust in human nature. But, unfortunately, Anthony was like intractable clay. He could not adjust to the school he was forced to go to. Here he re-enacted Greene's truancies. Anthony's life-graph is sketched by means of an interior monologue of Kate, his sister. She recalls her brother as a child:

> Anthony learning (the beating in the nursery, the tears before a boarding school) to keep a stiff upper lip, Anthony learning (the beating in the study when he brought home the smutty book with the pretty pictures) that you must honour other men's sisters. Anthony learning to love, with moderation. Anthony in Aden, Anthony in Shanghai, Anthony farther away from me than he had ever been. Anthony making good. Yes, he loved Anthony, and he ruined Anthony and he was tormented by Anthony until the end.[28]

The last sentence with "he" representing Anthony's father brings out the painful tragedy of the generation gap. The father's love has only an adverse effect and destroys the son. It falls like a blight on his soul which is barred from an insight into parental love. This same relationship is touched upon by E.M. Forster in his book, *Where Angels Fear to Tread.* Describing Gino, the Italian, who is shown caressing his son, Forster writes.

> The man was majestic, he was part of Nature; in no ordinary love scene could he ever be so great. For a wonderful physical tie binds the parents to the children; and by some sad, strange irony, it does not bind us children to our parents. For if it did, if we could answer their love not with gratitude but with equal love, life would lose much of its pathos and much of its squalor, and we might be wonderfully happy.[29]

Anthony's future is also moulded by the school from which he ran away. A pre-vision of his later failure was the meeting with his sister Kate in the barn. Kate sent him back to the school to pick up the conventions, the manners of all the rest. Anthony could not imbibe the sophistication and genteelness fostered there and spent the rest of his life keeping up appearances. G.S. Fraser describes him as

> ... a pathetic product, in fact, of English snobbery, which will not allow him to be honestly, decently rather drably himself.[30]

Thus vain, egoistic and dishonest, he turns out to be a latter-day version of a picaresque hero. Reflecting on his creation of Anthony, 25 years after the first publication of *England Made Me,* Greene writes in *Ways of Escape* that Anthony's character study is based on real life:

> I was quite satisfied with my portrait of Anthony. Hadn't I lived with him closely over many years. He was an idealised portrait of my elder brother, Herbert, and I had myself shared many of Anthony's experiences.[31]

Minty, in *England Made Me,* is another victim of school-life. He is a seedy nonentity, making a living by reporting on Krogh, the multi-millionaire. Although a loyal Harrovian, Minty relives continually the torments inflicted on him at school. It is reminiscent of Greene's alienation at school:

> A gang of school boys raced through Minty's mind, breaking up his pictures of Madonna and Child, jeering, belching, breaking wind.[32]

The pain and suffering he undergoes at school condition Minty to look at the world with contempt and mockery. The poison of hatred taken over a long period has made him, like Mithridates, immune to it. He has no hopes or ambitions and faces the world with malice:

> He had been broken in by parents, by schoolmasters, by strangers in the streets. Crooked and yellow and pigeon-

chested, he had his deep refuge, the inexhaustible ingenuity of his mind.[33]

In psychological terms, Minty is undeveloped and can only hit back against society by taking revenge. He, therefore, teases others. He teases the editor of his paper, Captain Gullie and the British Minister, Sir Ronald. At home, he identifies himself with a spider which he keeps trapped under the toothglass. The spider is Minty, clinging to wretched existence. Like the spider, too, Minty has developed an inane patience:

> And like the spider, he withered, blown out no longer to meet contempt, his body stretched doggo in the attitude of death, he lay there humbly tempting God to lift the glass.[34]

All along his life seems conditioned to attract betrayal and loneliness. What a disappointment it is to find that his only school friend, Anthony comes along with his girl-friend, Loo, to his apartment for the selfish purpose of using his bed. Eager to have friends, he recognises in Anthony his own seediness, but he is destined to remain lonely.

Conrad in *It's a Battlefield* is continually haunted by childhood memories of a traumatic type, whenever he is under stress. Subconsciously the stress triggers off memories of early experiences hidden in the psyche and makes him feel as helpless as he was as a victimized child. Associations of places in childhood surface—the smell of anthracite, the sound of drills, pictures of starved, naked children on a screen. In crises, he convicts himself of cowardice, lust, incompetence and ingratitude. As he walks to Battersea, thinking how he loved his brother who had been arrested for killing, and how he could help his brother out by a petition, the strain sets off stream-of-consciousness images in which his school and his present job get jumbled up:

> Into the darkness of the secondary school Conrad fell along without his brother, his name tossed across the asphalt— 'He's

called Conrad, Conrad, Conrad.' His brother sat in a steel cage driving through the rain; he earned three pounds a week, Conrad sat at a desk aware of the hatred behind him, in the School, in the office, the cold recognition of his efficiency through the glass door of the headmaster's room, of the manager's room, Conrad earned six pounds a week.[35]

When his brother's wife, Milly talks to Conrad, he wonders about the possibilities of her taking any interest in him sexually. Then suddenly she leaves him, disappointed. His thoughts are:

> She can't think of me as a man. Conrad, it was the name he could almost believe that prevented it. His parents had no business calling him by such a name, the name of a seaman . . . so 'Conrad, Conrad, Conrad' had been flicked at him across the desks, across the asphalt yard, driving him into isolation.[36]

Frustration in trying to solve his brother's problem brings the same sense of responsibility on him as he felt when he was shown pictures of naked, thin, starving children by a missionary at his school:

> He seemed unable to think about his own death; anxiety was greater than fear; he seemed haunted by his responsibility for Milly. A missionary tapped the screen in the stove-heated schoolroom with a long pointer, begged with passion 'Look at these,' and the children stared back . . . only Conrad felt the unbearable responsibility for their starvation.[37]

His pity for Milly makes him think of sex which he realizes would be adulterous. The measure of guilt starts the same associations from childhood.

> Milly lying back across the bed, hungry and unhappy and reaching for him; his mind reeled away from it to reflections

of Milly, to a trodden slipper slapping the floor, to the smell of anthracite and sound of drills, to the starved naked children or the screen.[38]

Even when he is dogging the Commissioner of Police in order to kill him, his nerve gives way and associations surface:

He took his final aim at the Commissioner, at the Policeman in the witness box, at the jester outside the Berkeley, at the directors's nephew, at the manager, at the voices calling 'Conrad, Conrad' across the asphalt yard. . . .[39]

One strained moment is catenated with earlier incidents back to childhood. Krogh, the multimillionaire industrialist in *England Made Me,* was a penurious child in Chicago and struggled for survival as a youth. His later life is a craving for money, an attempt to compensate for the wretchedness of his childhood. When he remembers the wild duck his father shot in childhood, he links it now in his mechanically-ordered present, with the idea of an abandoned, half-submerged aeroplane. He subconsciously equates the dead duck with abandonment and his present is an attempt to avoid that fear.

Professor Benjamin Jowett of Greene's radio play for the B.B.C. entitled *The Great Jowett* (which was broadcast on Saturday, 6th May, 1939 and was produced and narrated by Stephen Porter), lives to see childhood ambitions fulfilled. He is one of Greene's few characters who do not fail in the worldly sense, but childhood sufferings still mould his reactions to life and he makes a continual commentary on the failure of the school system. Professor Benjamin Jowett, a fellow of Oxford, aspires for the Mastership of Balliol. But members of the selection committee, Paul and Ross feel Jowett is not qualified for this on the grounds that he studies German criticism (Hegel) and too much Plato. This thwarts his childhood ambition. He had cherished it since the days when as a child he had suffered a humiliation. He tells Andrews:

No, no Andrew. These are nightmares. There's nobody else they can elect. Do you know the first time I ever met a Master of Balliol? I was a schoolboy, up from St. Paul's for a scholarship (They used to call me Miss Jowett there). I came into the dining-room. I was so nervous. I left my cap on. Jenkins came in. 'Do my eyes deceive me,' he said, 'or do I see a gentleman in my dining-room with his cap on?' You know, Andrews, it took me years to forgive him that rebuff. It taught me to be careful. Young men are so sensitive. You will find one burning with indignation for some neglect of which you were profoundly unconscious. No. It never does to speak roughly to them. When I am master. . . .[40]

Jowett, however, does achieve his ambition and becomes Professor of Moral Theology. He has written "A Commentary on St. Paul's Epistles" which is blasphemous. Ross, a member of the selection committee for the Mastership of Balliol, thinks his work will raise a storm. Doctor Jowett, having denied the Catholic faith, is denounced, and summoned by the Vice-Chancellor to sign the Thirty-Nine Articles or lose his fellowship. Talking about his degradation at the hands of his detractors, he says:

It was a schoolboy degradation they put me to.[41]

Every injury is but a repetition of the first humiliation suffered as a child. And ambition is a means to compensate for it, a desire to show "The Others" that one is worthwhile. Jowett becomes, in spite of his enemies, Master of Balliol. His "Plato" is published and Balliol Hall is built—his thumbmark is fossilized in stone in the College forever. At the gathering of the great Balliol people of the past, when he was receiving recognition from the Archbishop of Canterbury as "the statesman, the poet, the churchman" it might have seemed his day of triumph, but childhood shortcomings lurked in him. He tells his valet:

You know, Mathew, no day passes when I don't feel the

defects of early education. I was never taught how to play at chess or even at billiards, and it seems too late now. Do you think I could learn to waltz?[42]

There is another category of anti-heroes in Greene's works who are grave victims of childhood deprivations, and traumatic experiences have left permanent scars on their lives turning them to a life of crime.

Pinkie Brown or the Boy of *Brighton Rock* is a creation of "the evil in propria persona" which Greene saw as a child in school in the boy called Carter and in the town of Berkhamstead. The stunted product of a Brighton slum, Pinkie is steeped in delinquency. From the poverty and squalor of his childhood, he has graduated to an underworld of crime and violence. One day, passing through Nelson Place, the slum that was his birthplace, he feels an obscure shame because, for him, every step is a retreat into the dreary and dingy past." As he asks Rose's parents for her hand in marriage, he looks around at the fetid slum and is filled with disgust. He reflects:

Nobody could say he hadn't done right to get away from this, to commit any crime.[43]

Thus his neglected childhood in a slum has resulted in an anarchic adolescence. A pride in being ruined inspires all his actions and if thwarted or insulted by anyone, the poison of world-hatred twists in his veins:

He was going to show the world. They thought because he was only seventeen . . . he jerked his narrow shoulders back at the memory that he'd killed his man.[44]

A childhood of deprivations leads to a life of megalomaniac fancies in which he sees himself as a conqueror with an army of razors behind him. At such times his breast "ached with the effort to enclose the whole world." In Pinkie's life we may invert the

Wordsworthian concept of childhood. Pinkie trails the horrors of his childhood behind him. Enid Starkie says:

> Pessimism, despair and violent death follow inevitably on early corruption.[45]

Pinkie's whole personality is conditioned by the experiences in a wretched slum. The earliest scenes he was exposed to here have become the leit-motif of his life. These scenes include violence, crime, poverty and lust. He describes his slum to Rose, his girl friend:

> It's gaol, it's not knowing where to get some money. Worms and cataract, cancer . . . children being born. It's dying slowly.[46]

This is a picture of modern urban slums where among the filth and debris, moral degradation is born. In such slums the world of nature and human relationship is non-existent and the neglected child dies of "marasmus" or lack of love and stroking. Those who survive are predisposed to an angry lust for vengeance and the struggle for survival by evil means. Today's child of the slum, like Pinkie remains undeveloped psychologically. Pinkie has lived in hell all his growing up years and cannot even conceive of goodness.

> A brain was capable only of what it could conceive, and it couldn't conceive what it had never experienced; his cells were formed of the school playground, the dead fire, the dying man in the St. Pancras' waiting room, his bed at Billy's and his parents' bed. An awful resentment stirred in him—why shouldn't he have had his chance like all the rest, seen his glimpse of Heaven if it was only a crack between the Brighton walls.[47]

Early life and circumstances had left only one alternative for Pinkie—a life of evil. He had reached a point of no return, so steeped in crime he had become. He had avowed himself to the creed of Satan and was destined for damnation at the end of a chain corollary of crimes. Since society had abandoned him, he would avenge himself by falling in league with Satan. "Credo unum Satanum." Sadism acts as an emollient to his tortured spirit. He kills Hale and Spicer and designs the fake suicide pact to get rid of Rose. Pinkie becomes evil in personification and indulges in wanton cruelty like pulling off the wings of a leather jacket, crushing a moth out of existence under his shoe and pushing a blind man out of his way. Finally all that matters is a maniacal lust for murder that appeases his injured spirit.

> No more human contracts, other people's emotions washing at the brain—he would be free again: nothing to think about but himself. Myself: the word echoed.[48]

Pinkie is naturally possessed by the Devil himself. This Devil represents all the regrets and frustrations of a lost childhood. It is the very fabric of evil that his brain is composed of. Graham Greene says that Pinkie's misanthropy springs from:

> an egotism so complete that you could believe that something inhuman, supernatural was working there through the poor devils it had chosen.[49]

Pinkie's angst is the result of his voluntary estrangement from God. His alienation from society and his extraordinary saga of crime is the result of an anxious longing for a lost ideal, for an opportunity missed in childhood. He was in a choir once and wanted to be a priest. He sometimes murmurs snatches of the liturgy donis nobis pacem in an off-key voice in which

> a whole lost world moved; the lighted corner below the organ, the smell of incense and laundered surplices, and the music.[50]

In music he finds a vent for pent-up disappointments and

frustrations. Music conjures up a wish-world. His life may be an apt illustration for the opening lines of T.S. Eliot's poem, "Burnt Norton":

> Footfalls echo in the memory. Down the passage which we did not take. Towards the door we never opened.[51]

Pinkie's recollection of a missed opportunity to become a priest, faintly echoes a passing desire in Greene, when as a young man he was emotionally disturbed and was looking for a prop in religion. He had just been converted to Catholicism and he reflects about this in his autobiography:

> I remember very clearly the nature of my emotion as I walked away from the Cathedral: there was no joy in it at all, only sombre apprehension... suppose I discovered in myself what Father Trollope had once discovered, the desire to be a priest. ... At that moment it seemed by no means impossible. Only now after more than forty years, I am able to smile at the unreality of my fear and feel at the same time a sad nostalgia for it, since I lost more than I gained when the fear belonged irrevocably to the past.[52]

The Greene childhood syndrome is worked out in full in Pinkie's life: evil followed by failure, frustration and finally the death-wish. Pinkie despairs of any grace or forgiveness from God or freedom from the vicious circle of sin.

> He felt constriction and saw hopelessly out of reach—a limitless freedom: no fear, no hatred, no envy. It was as if he were dead and were remembering the effect of a good confession, the words of absolution; but being dead it was a memory only—he couldn't experience contrition—the ribs of his body were like steel bands which held him down to eternal unrepentance.[53]

Towards the end of the novel, as he drives out of Brighton with Rose, he feels grace reaching for him like,

> the pressure of gigantic wings against the glass and he withstands it with all the bitter force of the school bench, the cement playground, the Pancras waiting room.[54]

The lost childhood fights bitterly with grace. Pinkie is rushed along the chain reaction of events to his doom. We are left with a sense of compassion for the boy whose crippled childhood has incapacitated him from carrying adult responsibilities.

The mercenary murderer, Raven, anti-hero of *A Gun for Sale* (1936), belongs to the same class as Pinkie and represents

> a shadowy penumbra of unrealized possibilities, of might-have-beens.[55]

Both Pinkie and Raven have wounds that have never healed since childhood and which develop into an angoise metaphysique in later life.

Raven carries the wretchedness and poverty of his early life which stigmatize him with evil forever. He tells Anne, who is the only person in whom he feels an urge to confide, that a man is born with evil and the conditions of early life nurture it.

> It was like you carry a load around with you; you were born with some of it because of what your father and mother were and their fathers—seems as if it goes right back, like it says in the Bible about their sins being visited, then when you're a kid the load gets bigger: all the things you need to do and can't, and then all the things you do. They get you either way.[56]

Raven's burden calls to mind, besides the biblical allusion, the genetic theory which states that traits are inherited from immediate parents and sometimes from earlier ancestors. If the criminal traits of ancestors recur, they are termed "atavism." In this discussion, the idea of childhood is broadened to include not only man's early life from birth, but also the sins of Adam and Eve, the earliest prototypes of the childhood of mankind itself.

Traumatic scenes in Raven's early life have left deep scars on his character. His father was hanged and his mother cut her own throat. He saw his mother bleeding across the kitchen-table.

> He'd done some ugly things in his time, he told himself, but he'd never been able to equal that ugliness. Some day he would. The idea of a home is a place of suffering, not of love or happiness. He was brought up in one of His Majesty's own homes ... solitary confinement for a kid that's caught talking in the chapel, and the birch for almost anything you do. Bread and water. A sergeant knocking you around if you try to lark a bit.[57]

Raven further reflects:

> This isn't a world I'd bring children into.[58]

Raven was born with a harelip and his parents could not afford a good, skilled surgeon. It was badly sewn up and gave him an ugly appearance. This ugliness obsesses him and conditions him to assert himself on the world by crime and violence. His lip is a badge of class. He is treated as a pariah. No man likes him and women turn away from him. He loves no one except a kitten which is oblivious of his ugliness. When people turn away from the sight of his deformity, he is filled with humiliation and is overcome by a violent paroxysm to kill. Dark and thin, he is a study in destruction. The hatred of the world has made him into a thin, murderous figure hunted by everyone. Raven knows that the ugly have no chance of winning anything in the world. He reflects on the wretchedness of circumstances that brought him into the world.

> They have a good time and what do they mind if someone's born ugly. Three minutes in bed or against a wall, and then a

lifetime for the one that's born.[59]

Like Pinkie, Raven wallows in sadistic egotism. His criminality is a defence hurled against man and God, both of whom have forsaken him. Crime for him is an escape, a vengeance on the merciless cruelty of his childhood. Crime appeases his tortured mind. As he shoots Mr. Davis, he feels he is exterminating in the victim the corruption and injustice of the world in general:

> Raven shot him. With despair and deliberation he shot his last chance of escape, plugged two bullets in where one would do, as if he were shooting the whole world in the person of stout moaning bleeding Mr. Davis. And so he was, for a man's world is his life and he was shooting that: his mother's suicide, the long years in the home, the race-course gangs, Kite's death and the old man's and the old woman's.[60]

Raven is not spared the usual end in a Greene syndrome—death. Anne, the only person in the world who had found a place in his heart, to whom he could confide, betrays him to her fiancé, Detective Sergeant Mather.

> He had been marked from birth for this end, to be betrayed in turn by every one until every avenue into life was safely closed; by his mother bleeding in the basement, by the chaplain at the home, by the soft kids who had left it with him, by the shady doctor off Charlotte Street.[61]

About forty-two years after the creation of Pinkie and forty-four years after the creation of Raven, Greene was still obsessed with the theme of childhood wounds. Reflecting on these two criminal anti-heroes, Greene writes in *Ways of Escape* (1980):

> Raven the killer seems to me now a first sketch for Pinkie in *Brighton Rock*. He is a Pinkie who has aged but not grown up. The Pinkies are the real Peter Pans—doomed to be juvenile for

> a lifetime. They have something of a fallen angel about them, a morality which once belonged to another place. The outlaw of justice always keeps in his heart the sense of justice outraged. His crimes have an excuse and yet he is pursued by the others. The others have committed worse crimes and flourish. The world is full of Others who wear the masks of success, of a Happy Family. Whatever crime he may be driven to commit the child who doesn't grow up remains the champion of justice. 'An eye for an eye,' 'Give them a dose of their own medicine.' As children we have all suffered punishments for faults we have not committed, but the wound has soon healed. With Raven and Pinkie the wound never heals.[62]

The same undiminished preoccupation with "the lost boyhood of Judas" continues from his earliest book, *The Man Within* to the ones written later on. In his autobiography *A Sort of Life*, (1971) Greene himself plays a sort of Judas who rebels against his school curricula, and in *Ways of Escape* (1980), he reflects on the characters and themes of his books which emanate from his own early experiences.

James Wormold in *Our Man in Havana* (1958) and Arthur Rowe in *The Ministry of Fear* withdraw into a cocoon as soon as they are faced with the cruelties of adult life. Innocence was blighted early for them. Wormold's school-days strongly recall Graham Greene's own days at school. Even the names of his schoolmates are exactly the same as Greene's:

> The inefficient tortures of a school dormitory, torments with dividers practised by Collifax and Crandon.[63]

These experiences provoke Wormold to call childhood "the germ of all mistrust."

Middle-aged and physically unimpressive, he walks with a limp. He is unsuccessful in business, a sad, anxious man whose face reflects anxieties which are beyond the cure of a tranquiliser.

Deserted by his wife, Wormold has lived like a man in exile. Even after many years in Cuba, he feels he is a stranger there. His only companion is a German doctor, Haseslbacher. The failure of his marriage has left him mentally crippled and burdened with guilt. One must retain one's innocence, if one is to remain happy. Wormold says:

> Don't learn from experience, Milly. It ruins our peace and our lives.[64]

Wormold recalls a circus clown who fell every night into a bucket of whitewash and this act was never changed for each performance. According to Wormold that was the way to live. However, like the clown he grows into the butt of people's jokes, and cannot remain shielded from corruption. Arthur Rowe, hero of *The Ministry of Fear* lives his life nostalgically brooding over his childhood. He cannot muster courage to live in a world of adult complications. The Wordsworthian "shades of the prison house" fall heavily on him. He cannot bear adult responsibilities and relives the memories of simple days in childhood when he "trailed clouds of glory." He says:

> In childhood we live under the brightness of immortality—Heaven is as near and actual as the seaside. Behind the complicated details of the world stand the simplicities. God is good, the grown-up man and woman knows the answer to every question; there is such a thing as truth, and justice is as measured and faultless as a clock. Our heroes are simple: they are good swordsmen and they are never in the long run really defeated.[65]

Rowe's dictum on childhood reminds us of James Wormold in *Our Man in Havana* who advises Milly to retain innocence in order to be happy.

Rowe reads *The Old Curiosity Shop and David Copperfield* over and over again because he read them as a child and they contain no adult memories. He goes to the fete to recapture childhood associations. It calls back to him the pleasant vicarage gardens and girls in white summer frocks and the herbaceous borders and security. Rowe takes the cue for action in life from Charlotte Yonges' "The Little Duke" (Greene uses excerpts from this book to preface each chapter of *The Ministry of Fear* and to set the tone. This was one of the books that had interested Greene as a boy).

As a child Rowe had killed a rat whose back was broken. That scene filled him with the horrifying emotion of pity which affected him so much that he could never again suffer the pain of others. So overwhelming was the effect of the scene of the dead rat that he developed a "pain-phobia." When he grew up he had to go to the unthinkable extent of killing his own wife because he could not tolerate the physical pain she suffered from. It was to him euthanasia or mercy-killing.

He had learned before he was seven how dreadful pain was. He would not allow even a rat to suffer and this sensitivity to pain had made him unfit for practical living. He easily succumbed to other peoples' demands, if they only showed they were in dire need.

> People could always get things out of him by wanting them enough; it broke his precarious calm to feel that people suffered. Then he would do anything for them. Anything.[6]

His loss of innocence haunts him and surfaces in a dream in which he talks to his dead mother. He is horrified by what a child becomes, and what the dead must feel watching the change from innocence to guilt but is powerless to stop it.

Rowe is haunted with a sense of injustice too. The innocents must be saved and the guilty punished. He is one of the guilty and his guilt makes it impossible for him to distract or evade enemy agents. His involvement with them is a kind of unconscious self-retribution. The lieutenant in *The Power and the Glory* (1940) is haunted by a sense of injustice prevalent on earth. This hatred centres on the religion in his state and the false hopes it offered him as a child. His religion had done nothing to remove his miseries as a child and had left children in his state, Mexico, exposed to injustice.

> He wanted to destroy everything to be alone without any memories at all. Life began five years ago.[67]

He is inhibited by his childhood and his adult ambitions are moulded by his first experience:

> All his life had lain here: the syndicate of workers and peasants had once been a school. He had helped to wipe out that unhappy memory. . . . The new children would have new memories: nothing would ever be as it was. There was something of a priest in his intent observant walk—a theologian going back over the errors of the past to destroy them again.[68]

God and His Mercy to which people in his state cling, is anathema to him. The priest symbolises the pernicious influence of the Church. He wants to rid the world of all that is wretched and corrupt. Only children were fit to survive. They must not succumb to deprivations like he had.

> They deserved nothing less than the truth—a vacant universe and a cooling world, the right to be happy in any way they chose. He was quite prepared to make a massacre for their sakes. . . . He wanted to begin the world again with them, in a desert.[69]

All the characters discussed in this chapter (they do not exhaust the number created by Greene; there are other minor ones) are creations of Greene's own consciousness. Through them he relives the suffering, isolation and injustice of his early life, and through their emotions—vile and murderous, he calls attention to the grave dangers of a childhood gone astray.

Greene's characters show the continuity of consciousness from early life. People do not change. They only grow up accumulating memories. Ida Arnold in *Brighton Rock* reflects Grenee's view:

> Look at me. I've never changed. It's like those sticks of rocks: bite it all the way down you'll still read Brighton. That's human nature.[70]

In his reminiscences in *Ways of Escape,* Greene recalls Roberts, a friend of Oxford days. He remembers Roberts' idiosyncrasies—his crush on a beautiful maid they called Nefertiti. Later Greene met him when he was High Commissioner to Nairobi. Greene remarked that despite the passing of time, Roberts was still the same old man. Greene reflects:

> life that begins absurdly will go on absurdly to the end. The lines don't alter on the palm.[71]

NOTES

1. A.E., *Germinal*, quoted in "The Lost Childhood," *Collected Essays* by Graham Greene, The Bodley Head, London, 1969, p. 19
2. Montessori. Maria. *The Secret of Childhood,* Orient Longman, New Delhi, 1978, pp. 162-63.
3. *The Times Literary Supplement,* No. 3629, 17th Sept. 1971.
4. Kubie L.S., "The Neurotic Process as the Focus of Physiological and Psychoanalytic Research" in *The Journal of Mental Sciences*, Vol. 104, No.435 (1958), p. 62.
5. Greene, Graham, *A Sort of Life*, Penguin, London, 1974, p. 60.
6. Ibid.
7. Ibid., p. 61.

8. Ibid., p. 45.
9. Greene, Graham, "The Lost Childhood," in *Collected Essays*, Eyre and Spottiswoode, p. 17.
10. Greene, Graham, *A Sort of Life*.
11. Benet, William Rose, "Greene's *The Power and the Glory*," *The Saturday Review*, 30 March, 1940, p. 5.
12. Greene, Graham, *A Sort of Life*, p. 54.
13. Greene, Graham, *Ways of Escape*, Bodley Head, London, 1980, p. 174.
14. Greene, Graham, *A Sort of Life*.
15. Ibid., p. 74.
16. Wilson, Colin, *Beyond the Outsider*, Pan Books, London, 1962, p. 217.
17. Greene, Graham, *A Sort of Life*, p. 174.
18. Ibid., pp. 95-96.
19. Greene, Graham, *The Gamble* in *Babbling April*, Oxford, 1925, p.16.
20. Greene, Graham, "The End of the Party" from *Twenty-One Stories*, New York, 1954, p. 23.
21. Greene, Graham, *The Man Within*, Heinemann, London, 1950, p. 186.
22. Ibid., p. 10
23. Ibid., p. 33.
24. Ibid., p. 153.
25. Ibid., p. 147.
26. Ibid.
27. Ibid.
28. Greene, Graham, *England Made Me*, Heinemann, London, 1955, p. 72.
29. Forster. E.M., *Where Angels Fear to Tread*, Penguin, London, 1978., p. 125.
30. Fraser, G.S.. *The Modern Writer and His World*, Penguin London, 1964, p. 88.
31. Greene, Graham, *Ways of Escape*, Bodley Head, London, 1980, p. 37.
32. Greene, Graham, *England Made Me*, Heinemann, p. 9.

33. Ibid., p. 91.
34. Ibid., p. 147.
35. Greene, Graham, *It's a Battlefield,* William Heinemann, London, 1956, p. 97.
36. Ibid., p. 164.
37. Ibid., p. 233.
38. Ibid. p. 234.
39. Ibid., p. 264.
40. Greene, Graham, *The Great Jowett,* a radioplay for B.B.C.,1939, p. 16.
41. Greene, Graham, *BrightonRock,* Heinemann, London, 1955, p. 10.
42. Ibid., p. 40.
43. Ibid., p. 45.
44. Ibid.
45. Starkie, Enid, *From Gautier to Eliot,* Hutchinson Co., London, p. 198.
46. Greene, Graham, *Brighton Rock,* p. 104.
47. Ibid., p. 306.
48. Ibid., p. 11.
49. Greene, Graham in *The Lost Childhood and Other Stories,* Eyre and Spottis Woode, London, 1954, p. 29.
50. Greene, Graham, *Brighton Rock,* p. 66.
51. Eliot, T.S., "Burnt Norton," *Four Quartets,* Faber and Faber, p. 25
52. Greene, Graham, *A Sort of Life,* p. 122.
53. Greene, Graham, *Brighton Rock,* pp. 239-40
54. Ibid., p. 322.
55. Harvey, A.J., *Character of the Novel,* Chatto Windus, London, 1966, p. 147.
56. Greene, Graham, *A Gun for Sale,* Heinemann (Library Ed.), London, 1959, p. 160.
57. Ibid., p. 136.
58. Ibid.
59. Ibid., p. 150.
60. Ibid., P. 219.

61. Ibid,. p. 221.
62. Greene, Graham, "Ways of Escape," p. 72.
63. Greene, Graham *Our Man in Havana,* Heinemann, London, 1960, p. 55.
64. Ibid., p. 60.
65. Greene, Graham, *The Ministry of Fear,* Heinemann, London (Library Ed.), 1960, p. 102.
66. Ibid., p. 26.
67. Greene, Graham, *The Power and the Glory,* Heinemann, London, 1940, p. 20.
68. Ibid., p. 102.
69. Ibid., p. 25.
70. Greene, Graham, *Brighton Rock,* p. 77.
71. Greene, Graham, *Ways of Escape,* p. 38.

The Mortmain of the Past

> *Was there a couch, the stock-subject of so many jokes? I can't remember. I would begin to read out my dream, and he would check my associations with his watch. Afterwards he would talk in general terms about the theory of analysis, about the mortmain of the past which holds us in thrall.*[1]

The passage above from Greene's autobiography describes the psycho-analysis he underwent at the age of sixteen. His father was perturbed by his unusual behaviour and melancholic depression at school, and his continual truancies and sent him to the analyst, Kenneth Richmond in London. Greene further recalls his days with the analyst in the autobiography:

> My life with him did me a world of good . . . as Freud wrote, 'much is won if we succeed in transforming hysterical misery into common unhappiness.'[2]

It appears, therefore, that Greene was impressed by his experience of psycho-analysis, although the good effects and the general euphoria wore off like the after-effects of strong drugs. Greene employs in his works, techniques similar to those used in psycho-analysis. His characters unreel their past by interior monologue of the stream-of-consciousness type in which images shuttle back and forth, mixing the present with the past and retracing memories back to childhood where the root causes of their mental problems lie buried. Like in psycho-analysis, Greene's characters have dreams which are jumbled up images of the past, usually childhood experiences of trauma in thin disguise.

One basic difference between Greene's method of character-analysis and the clinical method of the psychiatrist is that while Greene's anti-heroes do not regain normalcy or freedom from the tyranny of the past, the patients in a series of psycho-analytical seances are usually helped to achieve some measure of happiness. The anti-heroes of Greene's novels do not take positive steps to correct the lacunae in their lives. We have seen that they indulge in brooding on the misfortunes of childhood which leads to an accumulation of bitterness and despair.

Greene's adolescent experience of undergoing psycho-analysis influenced his own technique of characterization.

Dreams have always held great significance for Greene in his own life and in his novels. He keeps a dream diary describing 800 dreams. In a recent interview printed in *The Sunday Statesman* of India, Greene recalls two prophetic dreams he had early as a child and which he related to a psycho-analyst:

> When I was a child of six, I had a dream which I can still remember: an enormous wave and a ship sinking. And that was on the night of the Titanic disaster. And, then in the period when I was psycho-analysed, I had another direct dream of the sea and that again was on the night when a ship went down in the Irish Sea with its passengers. . . .[3]

Through dreams, Greene's characters are in close and continual contact with their sub-conscious minds. There are more than sixty dreams in his works. They are meant to transplant the reader over the subliminal border where childhood memories lie stored up. In *The Ministry of Fear*, Arthur Rowe dreams that he is a little child who has killed a rat, but in the dream itself, he tells his mother that he has killed his wife. His mother laughs saying that her boy would not kill anyone. The illogical sequences of the dream may be interpreted in the light of Rowe's life. As a boy, he had broken the back of a rat. The scene had made him very sensitive to pain and as an adult he was not able to see human beings suffering. His wife's suffering, therefore, had led him to decide on euthanasia or mercy-killing to rid her of the pain. His mother's assurance in the dream that she could not think he would kill anyone may be a type of wish-fulfilment in which he wants his act of killing his wife to be approved.

In *A Gun for Sale,* Raven's dreams are the symbols of evil that he saw as a child—his mother's suicide, his father's death and his unhappy life in an orphanage.

Greene's use of interior monologue or stream-of-consciousness has been precisely illustrated earlier in this book where characters are described thinking. A moment of crisis or tension triggers off memories and associations—the past is linked to the present and a causal relationship established between different events. The short, staccato sentences are like flashes of memory lighting up the past where the seed of disturbance lies. For instance, Anthony, a marred product of his school from where he played truant, recalls his early days in *England Made Me:*

> I was frightened and father was ill and Kate came. Pale-green dormitory walls and the cracked bell ringing for tea . . . and then silence, like heaven, and I was alone until Kate came. .

The study of childhood memories is at the base of modern psychiatry. Modern schools of psycho-anaysis like the Transactional Analysis School, so popular in the West, believe that every man has a recording-system in the brain which stores up early memories. These recordings of experience keep replaying in later life, controlling and influencing human behaviour. Childhood, thus, contains the secret switches which trigger off associations that condition man's reactions to life later on. We saw that the anti-heroes of Greene's novels are tyrannized by early memories of trauma and phobia. They continually curse their existence which is the mutilated product of a lost childhood.

The role played by memory in an adult's life has been established by Dr. Wilder Penfield, a neuro-surgeon at McGill university in Montreal. During the course of brain surgery, he touched the tempora cortex of the patient with an electric current transmitted through a galvanic probe. The patient was fully conscious and able to talk. The neuro-surgeon heard amazing things from the patient. The stimulating electrode could force back recollections from the patient's memory. Not only past events were recalled in detail, but also the feelings associated with them. Penfield writes:

> The subject feels again the emotions which the situation originally produced in him, and he is aware of the same interpretations, true or false, which he himself gave to the experience in the first place.[5]

Related to the important role played by memory, is the Freudian theory that a psychologically disturbed patient can recover mental health if the memory of early events causing the disturbance is traced out. This is the work of psycho-analysts at the Couch—the humorous term used in the West for the bed in which the patient relaxes. According to one school of psycho-analysis—the Transactional Analysis or T.A. school, each man has three types of Ego states fixated in early life. These are termed Parent, Adult and Child. These are not to be confused with their literal meanings. Paul Drego, an Indian T.A. expert explains their meaning in T.A. terms:

> Each ego state has a system of feelings which is related to a set of behaviour patterns. Ego states are not roles but psychological realities. Parent Ego States resemble those of parental figures, Adult Ego States are the self's objective dealing with reality; and Child Ego States are those fixated in early childhood. That is your Parent indicates that you are responding as one of your parents with the same gestures, words and feelings etc. 'That is your Adult' means you have made an independent assessment of the situation in an objective manner. 'That is your Child' means your reaction is the same as it would have been when you were a very little boy or girl.

Parent, Adult and Child are modelled after and not synonymous with parent, adult, child.

A man's Ego states are "fixated" in early childhood in the form of memories. These memories are recorded in the subconscious and so as to say "replay" in later life. The Ego States determine how a man will react to situations and the set pattern of reactions is called in T.A., a life-script. Transactional Analysis is actually an applied form of Freud's theories. The great T.A. exponents Eric Berne, Thomas Harris, Muriel James have simplified the abstruse terms used by Freud. Freud's fundamental theory was that three warring factions existed in man's unconscious. The tentative names he gave them were: the Superego which is the restrictive controlling force, the Id or Instinctual drives and the Ego, which acts as a referee in enlightened self-interest. The approximate T.A. Counterparts to Freud's three states of mind are—Parent for Superego, Child for Id and Adult for Ego.

Each Ego State in Transactional Analysis, consists of various patterns of behaviour learnt early in life. Thus Parent Ego State includes critical behaviour, admonishments, do's and don'ts coming from parents and parent figures like guardians, society, teachers etc. The Adult Ego State is the individual's own discrimination, judgement and attitudes to situations as fixed in childhood after the intellect started functioning at about the age of five. The Child Ego State has both a positive and a negative aspect. In the positive aspect it includes creative talents, the power to enjoy life and to respond freely as in childhood. In the negative aspect, it includes reactions of fear, anger, hate, frustration etc. This negative aspect is also called the Adapted Child.

We may analyse the characters of Greene's novels in the light of the research done by psycho-analysis of the Transactional School. We have delineated Greene's anti-heroes earlier. All these characters are abnormal and unhealthy in nature since they show regressive behaviour and their actions leave a negative effect on their surroundings. They all have one psycho-analytical trait in common. Their Adult Ego States, or that part of their mind and intellect that makes decisions and judgements is seriously impaired leading to a confused logic in their thinking. There are two ways in which the Adult Ego State is "contaminated" or influenced in its reactions.

One, the Adult Ego State is strongly influenced by feelings of fear, anger or hatred coming from the Adapted Child of the character. That is to say, the character reacted to life around him as a child primarily with these negative emotions and the memories of these reactions replay continually in later life misleading and confusing the judgements of the Adult Ego State. The second way in which the Adult Ego is "contaminated" is by the presence of a strong Parent Ego in the character. Thus the parent or parent-figure, may it be society or school treated the child badly and gave him a very poor self-estimate which he fulfils by playing a negative role in society.

Francis Andrews of *The Man Within* is continually living a life in which reactions come mainly from the Adapted Child. Fear and hatred were his earliest reactions to his father's bullying. His father beat up his mother too and forced him to go to school and learn tough subjects only because he wanted to boast of his progeny. His decision to betray his father's gang of smugglers to the Assizes comes from an Adult Ego contaminated by early fears of the sea and the hatred for his father. He tells the Assizes that the reason for betraying his father's gang was:

> . . . because I had a father whom I hated and he was always being put before me as a model. . . . I was afraid of being hurt and I hated the sea and the noise and the danger. . . .[7]

His poor self-estimate is the judgement assessed by his Parent Ego. As a child, the smugglers provoked his inferiority complexes by saying:

> How could such a mountain bring forth such a mouse?[8]

Elizabeth, whom he loves, is killed because he goes away for the night to enjoy the body of Lucy. This leaves Elizabeth unprotected. Andrews' logic for her death is:

> His father had made him a betrayer and his father had slain Elizabeth. . . . I am my father, he thought, and I have killed her.[9]

A psycho-analyst would read this interior monologue or life-script as coming from an Adult Ego strongly contaminated by the Parent Ego.

Anthony Farrant of *England Made Me* goes through life by deceit and false credentials. He sports a Harrovian tie he is not entitled to. He cannot stick to one job and moves from failure to failure. As a child, he was loved by his father who wanted to give him the education for a gentleman, but Anthony could not by temperament adjust to his school and kept playing truant. The conflicts between his temperament and his father's insistence that he acquire the manners of the school resulted in an Adult Ego contaminated by dictates from the Parent Ego. He concludes for himself: I must play the gentleman even if I cannot be one. This leads to a character of false pretensions. When he sides with the workers in Krogh's establishment, he is "playing" the good man by serving the underdog. However, he does not calculate the risks and it brings about his death.

Conrad Drover in *It's a Battlefield,* has a strong Adapted Child. That is to say, he responded with fear and anger to children teasing him at school and across the asphalt road. Whenever under tension, in a crisis, his judgements are impaired by associations of fear and anxiety. His despair regarding his brother who is in prison, his concern for his sister-in-law, Milly, his decision to shoot the Assistant Commissioner of Police are reactions from his Adapted Child—associations of fear and alienation always surface whenever he is in crisis. His self-estimate is poor. He considers his name a sign of failure. He says that his parents had no business calling him by that name. He convicts himself of failure—failure to get justice for his brother who is in prison and to arrange his sister-in-law's life.

These reactions to himself and his problems show an Adult Ego (the power that makes judgements) strongly influenced by the Adapted Child in him.

Minty of *England Made Me,* Pinkie of *Brighton Rock* and Raven of *This Gun for Sale* have Adult Ego States strongly contaminated by Parent Ego States. Parents and parent-figres like society and school abandoned them in childhood. Minty was jeered at school and Pinkie and Raven were brutalized or abandoned as children by parents and society. Their Parent Ego always says to them: "You are bad and negligible." Their Adult Ego passes the same judgement on others. Thus Minty teases people like the British Minister; Pinkie and Raven kill people. Their collection of early childhood memories is marked by toughness and cruelty and these now influence their reactions to people around. They have permission from the Parent Ego States to be tough and cruel. Doctor Jowett, the character of the play of the same name desires fame in life. He strives hard to become Master of Balliol. He fights against odds to gain this prestigious position. The Selection Committee is against him, yet he perseveres. The decision to achieve his ambition with such fierceness comes from his Adapted Child. As a child, he recalls a humiliation he suffered at the hands of a schoolmaster. He, therefore, considers it a humiliation or a relegation to a lower status not to achieve a highly prestigious rank in the university. In other words, he is working to compensate for the sense of inferiority provoked in him as a child.

Krogh, the rich industrialist in *England Made Me* suffered from poverty as a child. His Adapted Child is a memory of those unhappy days and he decides to wallow in money, to do away with deprivation forever even at the cost of human values.

Arthur Rowe in *The Ministry of Fear* decides issues for himself from a strong Adapted Child State. As a child, he had killed a rat, which left him very sensitive to pain. That is to say, he could not see people suffer at all. That early experience made him give in to people who demanded things from him. When his wife was in great pain, he decided to kill her on grounds of euthanasia or mercy-killing. His reaction to his wife's pain is the same as his reaction to the pain of the dying rat. Rowe cannot carry adult responsibilities. He is afraid of the world around him. He reads the books he read as a child and likes to brood on his childhood. He is reacting to life constantly from his Adapted Child which contains memories of the fear of pain.

James Wormold in *Our Man in Havana* was tortured at school by bullies. He reacts to life from his Adapted Child. He is full of anxieties and guilt—the same reactions generated in him by early experience.

The Lieutenant in *The Power and the Glory* has early memories of suffering children. His Adapted Child influences his reactions to life and moulds his reactions to life around. He wants to destroy everything that could not take care of the happiness of children. He wants to destroy the priests who represented a failed ideal.

NOTES

1. Greene, Graham, *A Sort of Life,* Penguin, London, 1971, p. 74.
2. Ibid., p. 79.
3. Sikiorski, Radek, "The Heart of the Matter," in *The Sunday Statesman*, May 27, 1984, p. 8.
4. Greene, Graham, *England Made Me,* Heinemann, London, 1955, p. 14.
5. Penfield, W., "Memory Mechanism" in A.M.A. *Archives of Neurology and Psychiatry*, 67, 1952, p. 178.
6. Drego, Paul, *Towards the Illumined Child,* The Grail, Bombay, 1979, pp. 4-5.
7. Greene, Graham, *The Man Within*, Heinemann, London, 1950, p. 153.
8. Ibid., p. 202.
9. Ibid., p. 238.

Original Sin: Sexual Guilt and Frustration

When Adam and Eve broke God's commandment in the Garden of Eden and ate the forbidden fruit, they were suddenly made aware of shame and sexual sin and covered themselves in leaves. That was the original sin committed by man in the childhood of evolution and for that his progeny was to suffer. Such is the story in the Bible and the story may be an allegory of man's downfall because of one wrong step in early life. This step may have been made by society, by parents or by the whole educational machinery.

Most of Greene's anti-heroes suffer from the taint of original sin. They are all victims of sexual desire or lust. Yet they look upon the libidinous act as abhorrent. They are joined to women by "a painful coitus."[1] They never embrace freely, yet they are carried away by the need for lascivious satisfaction. And after the sex-act they are overcome by a sense of sin. Moral compunctions act as barriers to the enjoyment of their natural, basic functions. As a corollary to this experience they inevitably fail in love.

What is the origin of this ambivalent attitude to love in Greene's books? I think it is directly or indirectly related to Greene's development in early life and adolescence. The moral indoctrination to which he was exposed was faulty. It was based on inhibitions regarding sex. It was not informed by that broad outlook to sex that modern education inculcates. Thanks to the findings of the psychologist Sigmund Freud, sex-education is considered a must in many centres of learning today. What a far cry it is today from the early thirties when Greene and other writers were brought up in prudery. Today, the balance in some countries has tipped to the other extreme leading to permissiveness in some cases and it does as much harm as in those days when education suppressed the thirst for knowledge and warped the sexual instincts. John Atkins in his study of Graham Greene remarks that a narrow outlook in sex was a general malaise of the thirties:

> One of the major criticisms made of the public school during the nineteen-thirties was that it warped the sexual instinct. No matter how sincerely the headmaster wished to adopt the progressive ideas to education and the organization of a boarding school, he was himself inhibited from any contact with new ideas by his insulated life, graduating from school to university and so back to school. As a result even the best headmasters still believed in their hearts that sex was dirty and acted on the assumption. They were guilty in the main of two misconceptions; that sex could never be pleasant or amusing, and that marriage is always sacred.[2]

Graham Greene was educated at Berkhamstead School where his father was headmaster. It was an atmosphere of puritanism in which this Anglican Protestant school was steeped. Talk of sex was taboo and children were shielded from any knowledge of the demon called sex. In his autobiography, *A Sort of Life*, Greene describes this with humorous intent:

> If I had known it, the whole future must have lain all the time along those Berkhamstead Streets. The High Street was wide as many a market square, but its broad dignity was abused after the first great war by the New Cinema under a green Moorish dome, tiny enough but it seemed to us then the height of pretentious luxury and dubious taste. My father who was by that time, headmaster of Berkhamstead School, once allowed his senior boys to go there for a special performance of the first "Tarzan" movies, under the false impression that it was an educational film of anthropological interest and ever after he regarded the cinema with a sense of disillusion and suspicion.[3]

The passage reveals that Greene's ideology was largely shaped by his training at Berkhamstead and that the social norms as represented by his father, looked upon the cinema as a symbol of "dubious taste." The cinema with its stimulating scenes was conducive to moral degradation. There was, in general, a puritanical revulsion of luxury or pleasure. Greene also mentions some of the strictures taken at school to guard contamination of the students' minds by anything pornographic. A strict censorship of books was kept by one Mr. Herbert. However these were the books that came from the students' homes. The censorship was not foolproof since it overlooked the books which were available in the school library—

> The danger lay in the source—home, where dwelt unreliable and uncelibate parents. Anything in the library was acceptable—even the inflammatory blank verse of Sir Lewis Morris from whom I later learned of the carnal loves of Helen and Cleopatra.[4]

Graham Greene points out a similar anomaly in the moral inculcation in another field. The serious no-nonsense attitude to sex failed:

> It was sexually a very pure house, there was no hint of homosexuality . . . but scatology was another matter, and I have disliked the lavatory joke from that age on.[5]

There were yet other regulations which sought to check immorality. Greene describes the school rules which seemed to be enforced interminably. Like the Roman Curia, these rules changed very slowly. The censorship of books from home which was strictly enforced like a customs examination was dropped with Mr. Herbert's retirement. But other regulations remained. Lavatories had no locks lest privacy be used for self-abuse:

> Lavatories without locks, where each newcomer, anxious to

perform his morning duty, had to call out, 'Number Off' in order to learn which of the compartments was empty, and the rule for Sunday walks which made certain that no one, under any circumstances would ever walk dangerously alone.[6]

When Greene was thirteen years of age, he continually escaped to the moors to run away from his boredom. Here in the Commons, he was ambushed by his elder sister, Molly, who led him back home. His father was perturbed and anxious about these escapades imagining them to be risque ventures into adolescent sex. Graham Greene says:

> I seem to remember my father sitting on the bed and interrogating me seriously and tenderly, and from that interrogation grew a whole comedy of errors. I suppose I complained of the general filth of my life at St. John's, meaning the unlocked lavatories, the continual farting of my companions-but he misunderstood me and believed I had been the victim of some ring of masturbation so that other investigations were now set on foot among the innocent inhabitants of St. John's. The truth was I had not yet discovered the pleasure of masturbation and didn't even know the meaning of the word, though my father in any case probably used some vague abstract expression which was equally applicable to breaking wind.[7]

Greene's view of life, even as a child was more mature than that of his schoolmates. This attitude to sex, besides being influenced by the moral inhibitions of school were also affected by his own natural temperament which was already too mature for his times. In 1934, he edited a selection of essays under the title, *The Old School.* The contributors like Elizabeth Bowen, L.P. Hartley, Arthur Calder-Marshall and Anthony Powel, often enjoyed their schooldays or at any rate failed to react positively against them. Greene limits himself to considerations of sex in public schools feeling that co-education would offer no better alternative.

A comradely no-nonsense-about-sex attitude between men and women is particularly repellent.[8]

This view of Greene shows that his early education resulted in a temperament that was unnatural. John Atkins says:

> When he had done a little coaching, he discovered he didn't like little boys. It is probable he never had liked them, had developed emotionally at a very early stage and chafed under school restrictions and the normally accepted mythos of boyhood. That is to say he had been boy enough to want to discover gold in Africa but not to find girls a kind of natural joke as were the lower classes for the Punch subscribers of that day.[9]

Greene stood apart from his childhood schoolfellows by virtue of his emotional maturity and he was generally a misogynist. But one cannot deny the fact that Greene was troubled by pricks of sexual desire, unconsciously enjoying them in early childhood and breaking into unabashed lusty longings at puberty. So, there was always this antithetical pull on his mind. On the one hand he pooh-poohed girls and yet on the other he succumbed to temptations whenever occasion arose or the demands of adolescence grew riotous. There was besides, always an element of secrecy in his discoveries about sex. The sense of sin and guilt weighed on him. We shall see how this same ambivalence characterizes his anti-heroes.

What does modern psychology reveal about the results of sexual repression? Most modern research in this line begins with Sigmund Freud. Not all later psychologists agree totally with Freud, but their discoveries are to a great extent dependent on his. In broad terms, they all agree that repression in the form of inhibitions or too many moral restrictions lead to deviations in later life. These deviations may be a type of neurosis, or a perversion. The traditional method of holding back the truth about sex or mutilating it is really harmful:

> The fable of the stork is often told to an audience that receives it with deep, though mostly silent mistrust. There are, however, two elements that remain undiscovered by the sexual researches of children: the fertilizing role of semen and the existence of the sexual orifice, the same elements incidentally in which the infantile organism is itself undeveloped. It therefore follows that the efforts of the childish investigator are habitually fruitless, and end in a renunciation which not infrequently leaves behind it a permanent injury to the instinct for knowledge. The sexual researches of childhood are always carried out in solitude.[10]

The "permanent injury to the instinct for knowledge" may take perverse turns or lead to psychoneurosis in adolescence. Social checks do not extinguish the thirst for sex-knowledge. It ferments in the subconscious and whenever the guardians of mental health are looking away, it breaks through in bawdy jokes, pornography and a frightened visit to the brothel. Freud confirms this again:

> We must not deceive ourselves as to the hypothetical nature and insufficient clarity of our knowledge concerning the processes of the infantile period of latency or deferment: but we shall be on firmer ground in pointing out that such an application of infantile sexuality represents an educational ideal from which individual development usually diverges at some point and often to a considerable degree. From time to time a fragmentary manifestation of sexuality which has evaded sublimation may break through; sexual activity may persist through the whole duration of the latency period until the sexual instinct emerges with great intensity at puberty.[11]

In Graham Greene's case the incidents of "fragmentary manifestation of sexuality" are described by Greene himself in his autobiography, *A Sort of Life*. The child Graham may have been embarrassed as a child on being kissed by a Miss Willis during his seventh birthday, and feared coming below the mistletoe during Christmas, but sexual brushes brought him hidden pleasure. Greene describes a war game he played early in which—

> scouting behind hedges, crawling along ditches, making heroic forays across an open space one experienced the first hint of sexual interest for the enemy—the girl on sentry duty in the stable yard.[12]

Further, Greene recalls having been taken to a revival of "The Admirable Crichton." The heroine, dressed in animal skin affected him deeply:

> Was it Cathleen Nesbitt who played the part? If so, those disturbed nights had been experienced not long before by Rupert Brooke. But it was not 'mother comfort' I sought even at that age. It was some years before I was again so sexually moved by a play, and then it was by Chistopher Sly. The beautiful actress who played with Matheson Lang and was his wife wore a long white silk night dress which proved just as exciting as the animal skins.[13]

While sexual stimulation was unavoidable, Greene disliked girls in general. He once told his elder sister Molly and through her, girls in general, "You are silly Molly. Girls are so silly. . . . Girls wouldn't know. They know nuffin'. Girls are always slow and always last."[14] This rather misogynistic attitude found its way into his short story, "The End of the Party." Here Francis Morton (probably young Greene himself) despises girls and is mortally afraid of being touched by any in games of hide and seek:

> Girls were like that. You didn't hear them coming. They slunk along like cats.[15]

The same emotion is echoed in Greenes' book *England Made Me* (1930) when describing Minty:

He didn't like girls, he couldn't have said it in words more plainly; tawdry little creatures, other people's sisters, their hats blocking the view at Lords.[16]

With the onslaught of puberty and adolescence, Greene's mind fermented with sexual desire. He recalls how he used one of his truancies from school for reading a sexually stimulating book:

> The days of Henty were over—my body was leading my brain in unfamiliar directions. I found extraordinary beauty and passion, I remember, in Sir Lewis Morris' 'Epic of Hades,' and perhaps I was reading lines like these spoken by Helen of Troy:
>
> 'Was it love
> That drew men to Paris? He was fair,
> I grant you fairer than a summer morn,
> Fair with a woman's fairness,
> Yet in arms
> A hero, but he never had my heart
>
> Today the lines seem pinchbeck, and yet they retain the secret smell of my hiding-place.[17]

Greene's mind broke through all the strangleholds of moral indoctrination as the demands of adolescence overpowered him. His autobiography wreaks with confessions such as this:

> Literature can have a far more lasting influence than religious teaching and my father's enthusiasm for Robert Browning was the bacillus of a recurring fever. The edition I still possess of the poems was given me by him as a confirmation present, but it was certainly not a belief in God that Browning confirmed. I had emerged from my psycho-analysis without any religious belief at all, certainly no belief in the Jesus of the chapel, and what I took from Browning, my father might well

have thought unhealthily selective. To recall today any phrase from the Sermon on the Mount I must open the New Testament to find the words, but some lines of Browning have stayed in my memory for fifty years and have influenced my life more than any of the Beatitudes:

> Better sin, the whole sin, sure that God observes;
> Then go live his life out!
> Life will try his nerves,
> When the sky, which noticed all, makes no disclosure,
> And earth keeps up her terrible composure.
> And the sin I impute to each frustrate ghost
> Is—the unlit lamp and the ungirt loin
> Though the end in sight was a vice I say.[18]

Robert Browning took Greene on a ride into:

> a region of adulteries, of assignations at dark street corners, of lascivious priests and hasty dagger thrusts, and of sexual passion far more heady than romantic love.[19]

Such, in fact was to become the leit-motif of many of Greene's novels—A world of passion and crime is painted in them. Greene's autobiography becomes nostalgically eloquent as it recreates the fever of those bygone days:

> As we grow old we are apt to forget that state of extreme sexual excitement in which we spent the years between 16 and 20. There was a musical comedy in the early twenties called 'The Cabaret Girl' in which Miss Dorothy Dickson starred. To-day it would seem, I suppose, as comic as 'The Boy Friend,' but during my first year after leaving school, I saw it six times, and every time but one in a state of continuous physical excitement. . . . We lived in those days continuously with the sexual experience, we had never known; we talked, we dreamt, but it was always there, and yet, when I came to

write it was sentimental verse or prose fantasies which leaked from the pen.[20]

Greene's anti-heroes suffer from the pulls of sexual desire just like he did as a child and adolescent. Like him they give in to passion not because it is premeditated, but because of the demands of their lower self. And the outcome is generally guilt and a failure to continue the love. What are the origins of this guilt-complex in Greene's attitude or view? We have already elaborated the moral indoctrination of his school. The school ethics did not consider the psychological necessity of studying the problem of sex with students in an open, healthy manner and the result was guilty feelings. The 'Albatross' of Guilt must have hung on these students when they grew up and love could never be fructifying or consummated in their view. Bertrand Russell, the philosopher, explains this predicament in clear-cut terms:

> Many adults in their hearts still believe all that they were taught in childhood and feel wicked when their lives do not conform to maxims of the Sunday School. The harm done is not merely to introduce a division between the conscious reasoning personality; the Adult and the unconscious infantile personality or child; the harm lies also in the fact that the valid parts of conventional morality become invalidated along with the invalid parts. The danger is inseparable from a system which teaches the young, en bloc a number of beliefs that they are almost sure to discard when they become mature.[21]

Greene's early inhibited moral education was a common malaise of the thirties. Other writers like Isherwood and Auden could not escape the ineradicable stamp left by the public school of those times. For several of them the process was complicated by returning to the school world after leaving university, to earn a living by teaching in prep schools or public schools. So we find in the writing of the thirties the insistent presence of schools and schoolboys and schoolmasters as sources of imagery, theme and tone. Greene's contemporaries, Wystan Hugh Auden and Christopher Isherwood went to prep school, St. Edmund's at Hindhead, Surrey. In *Lions and Shadows* (1938) Isherwood provides a lively caricature account of Auden as a boy, already domineering and seemingly omniscient:

> To several of us, including myself, he confided the first naughty stupendous, breath-taking hints about the facts of sex. I remember him chiefly, for his naughtiness, his insolence, his smirking tantalizing air of knowing disreputable and exciting secrets. With his hinted forbidden knowledge and stock of mispronounced scientific words, pretentiously uttered, he enjoyed among us, his semi-savage schoolfellows, the status of a kind of witch-doctor.[22]

Isherwood's obsession is commonplace in the writings of the thirties, when the conventions and codes of the prep school and public school often used to convey serious social and political attitudes. Isherwood reflects Greene's own prurience as a schoolboy. Writing in *Lions and Shadows,* Isherwood says:

> I build up the day dream of a heroic school career, in which the central figure, the dream I, was an austere young prefect, called up unexpectedly to captain a bad house, surrounded by sneering critics and open enemies, fighting slackness, moral rottenness, grimly repressing his own romantic feelings towards a younger boy.[23]

Next we must consider the theme of failure in love in Greene's novels. As an adolescent schoolboy Greene realized the difficulty of entering into a successful love-affair with the girl one dreamt of. He recalls in his autobiography:

> What a mess those inexperienced years can be. Lust and boredom and sentimentality, a frightened longing for the

> prostitute in Jerym Street . . . an unreal romantic love for a girl with a tress of gold and a cousin who played tennis when it was almost too dark to see the ball—in that twilight world of calf love any number of girls can rehearse simultaneously a sentimental part which never reaches performance.[24]

Greene was to savour of frustration in an early love-affair. During the summer of 1923 (Greene was 17 then), Greene reluctantly joined his family at Sheringham on the Norfolk Coast. There was a governess for his younger brother and sister at Sheringham. Gradually his mind awoke to sexual possibilities. "The first time I looked at her with any interest was at the same time the coup de foudre." He saw her lying romantically on the beach and her skirt was up high so that he could see the tempting thigh. His flirtations with her went on. She did not mind it because it helped to while away the time. With the excuse of learning dancing, he danced with her and exchanged "half-kisses." But some time later she was engaged to a man working for Cables and Wireless in the Azores. The governess must have become romantically attached to him for she wept while divulging the fact of her engagement to him. The memory of that transient passion must have lingered long in Greene's mind and unconsciously it influenced the plot of a spy story he wrote in about his twenty-first year. In this story entitled. *A Sense of Security,* a young governess is found murdered in a country house, and the clues are too many and baffling for the police. A local priest who recognizes child psychology behind the clues, finds out the killer—a girl of twelve who had committed this crime because her beloved governess was in love with a man. Who was this twelve-year old girl? Greene himself? He confides to us in his autobiography:

> Now I can detect the various threads of my short experience which intermingled: my sister's governess, jealousy of the man she was to marry. . . .[25]

Further Greene reminisces about the nature of this adolescent love-affair in his autobiography:

> I was seventeen and terribly bored and in love with my sister's governess—one of those miserable, hopeless, romantic loves of adolescence that set in many minds the idea that love and despair are inextricable and successful love hardly deserves the name.[26]

These two words in juxtaposition— "love and despair" is the set pattern of the love-affairs and the relationship of the married couples in Greene's works.

In *Babbling April,* Greene's anthology of poems is a piece called "1930" which may be taken as a suitable preface to the description of the love-frustration theme in his novels.

> Then through the crumbling of some bread I'll ponder
> I'll ponder through the scraping of a plate
> How love which should have been a blaze of wonder
> Has been a dusty and untended grate.
> With crooked, grimy bars twisted asunder,
> Because its servant rose from sleep too late.[27]

The Love-affairs or sexual attitude of the following characters in Greene's works may be considered in the light of his own experiences.

1. Francis Andrews, Elizabeth and Lucy in *The Man Within.*
2. Conrad Drover, Milly and Kay Rimmer in *It's a Battlefield.*
3. Anthony Farrant, Kate and Loo in *England Made Me.*
4. Minty in *England Made Me.*
5. Pinkie Brown and Rose in *Brighton Rock.*
6. The Whiskey Priest and God in *The Power and the Glory.*
7. Major Scobie, Helen and Mrs. Louise Scobie in *The Heart of the Matter.*
8. Maurice Bendrix and Sarah Miles in *The End of the Affair.*
9. Fowler, Phuong and Plarr in *The Quiet American.*

10. Plarr, Clara and Fortnum in *The Honorary Consul.*
11. Myatt and Coral Musker in *Stamboul Train.*
12. Raven, Anne and Mather in *A Gun for Sale.*
13. Daintry, his wife and Castle in *The Human Factor.*

In almost all the books, there exists either a triangular or three-cornreed love-affair or a complementary two-way love. All are inane, self-defeating emotions leading to frustration. In fact they spring from Greene's established experiences in early life.

In *The Man Within,* Francis Andrews might have succeeded in finding a refuge in the pure and ennobling love for Elizabeth, but he is continually dragged down by his lower, sinful self and gives in to the lechery for Lucy's body. The demands of his animal self villify his motives for appearing as the witness for the prosecution. He reminds himself that he is there for Elizabeth's sake, but immediately after the scene, he goes off to spend the night with Lucy. Elizabeth is left to the mercy of the smugglers who torture her. "I've wallowed" he says describing his sexual pleasure with Lucy. But the inevitable consequence of sexual love in Greene protagonists is an overwhelming sense of guilt. Francis is overcome with a terror of going on soiling himself again and again and repenting in vain.

Andrews' love for Elizabeth stands out as rare in Greene's novels, because it is edifying and reassures Andrews that there is a possibility of real tender love. Her presence dispels the fear of falling into sin and conjures up a world of stable beauty and love:

> He thought of the seasons they would see together: of summer, blue sea, white cliffs, red poppies in the golden corn, winter to wake in the morning to see Elizabeth's hair across the pillow, her body close to his, and outside the deep, white silence of snow: spring again with restless hedgerows and the call of birds . . . and always the music of her voice which seemed to him in this new foolish drunken happiness more lovely than any instrument.[28]

In her presence even his sexual desires are elevated to pure love:

> There was a kind of mystery, in Elizabeth, a kind of sanctity which blurred and obscured his desire with love. Here was no love and no reverence. The animal in him could ponder her beauty crudely and lustfully, as it had pondered the charms of common harlots, but with the added spice of reciprocated desire.[29]

I find a strong resemblance between the sanctity of Elizabeth and the character of Graham Greene's mother as portrayed in his autobiography. In the early years when the child Greene's mind was forming an image of human types around him, Greene could not react positively to friends at school or teachers or his father and other relatives. It is only his mother who stands out as worthy of respect. His mother seemed to be the only pleasant influence of his childhood. In *A Sort of Life,* he recalls her with picturesque delight.

> I associate my mother with a remoteness which I did not at all resent, and with a smell of eau-de-cologne. If I could have tasted her I am sure she would have tasted of wheaten biscuits. She paid occasional state visits to the nursery in the School House, a large confused room which looked out of the flint church and the old cemetery, with toy cupboards . . . and my mother gained in my eyes great dignity from her superintendence of the linen-cupboard where a frightening witch lurked. . . . The wheaten biscuit remains for me a symbol of her cool puritan beauty—she seemed to eliminate all confusion, to recognize the good from the bad and choose the good. . . . When she was in an untroubled coma before death and I was watching by her bed, her long white plantagenet face reminded me of a crusader on a tomb.[30]

In Andrews' life, Elizabeth has the same beneficial influence, eliminating all confusion from his mind for a while and enthusing him with hope.

But the Greene syndrome must end in despair and the failure of love. Andrews fails his acid test as a lover. He cannot rescue Elizabeth from the smugglers. Tortured by the smugglers, Elizabeth kills herself, with the same knife that Andrews had left behind for her protection before he left for Lewes. Her death is the beginning of despair—a natural corollary of love.

In *It's a Battlefield,* love takes on the same overtones of stigmatized love, marred by the element of physical passion and lust. Conrad Drover wants to rescue his sister-in-law, Milly, from her suffering by giving her love and attention but the act of love is followed by a sense of irrevocable injury that they have done each other by committing adultery. Love escapes, leaving behind a residue of guilt and hatred. Conrad muses on the difference of his relationship with Kay Rimmer and with Milly. Both relationships are fraught with guilt:

> They call that lust and this is love. He meant the hate and the pain and the sense of guilt and the sound of crying in the graying room and sleeplessness.[31]

In Greene's novels, sexual love vitiates human relations instead of bringing people close to each other in consummation. It causes rifts and leaves a residue of guilt and frustration. After Conrad has made love to Kay Kimmer, he feels guilty of having "ditched" Milly. His love for Kay has only been a physical need—which leaves behind a residue of painful guilt.

> Before their bodies had known each other, they had been closely acquainted, they had even shared something; their nerves and their suspicion, in which Jim had no part at all. . . . He could believe that she loved him in a way; and that way, though it promised no satisfaction, was better than this shared lust, this shared ignorance of anything beyond a touch, a sense of physical closeness, a heat and a movement.[32]

Conrad Drover is tormented by a guilty secret. As he was

alone walking through the streets of London, he feels betrayed by his lower self, and forsaken. To rid himself of this oppressive guilt and hatred, Conrad falls back on Milly, but knows full well that the cycle of despair would repeat itself invariably—lust, guilt and frustration:

> The act which was to have been his armour against life, the secret inner pride . . . had betrayed him, had driven him along streets too many to count, had trailed him like a dusty coat behind the Assistant Commissioner. Milly, too, had betrayed him; she had given him the only thing he wanted, a thing he had never had the least hope of obtaining, and it proved something lovely over too quickly, weeping in the night, sleeplessness, condemnation, despair. He clenched his hands in a fury of useless hatred.[33]

In *England Made Me,* love is again treated as a tragic emotion, doomed to end abortively. Kate's love for her brother, Anthony, has unmistakable incestuous overtones. Anthony, however, cannot understand her advances as anything but sisterly love. Kate's love is, therefore, to remain unrequited passion. Kate's relationship with her employer, Krogh, is not love and the only sexual union she has with him is provoked by a visitor who reminds her of Anthony. Kate's sexual advances to her brother are signified in gestures like planting the lovers' pinch on Anthony's palm. Anthony, however, responds negatively:

> Love was not gratitude, love was not this dependence of the brain, this thought-reading, this inconvenience of shared pain; this was the unfortunate trick of being twins; love was fun, love was a good time, love was Annette, was Mabel.[34]

Kate's love has the handicap of a sister's relationship. It cannot win Anthony from Loo, who is "a recurrent itch of the flesh."[35] Kate's love is family affection, sharing of a lifetime of experiences, that is all. Frustration of love is the inevitable end.

Kate is forced to pray to save herself the pain of parting from Anthony.

Anthony is lost to her and gone. All he promises her is three pages of letters every Sunday.

In the same novel, sex receives a different treatment, in the character of Minty. Sex becomes an emotion that stirs disgust and revulsion. The human body is a container of disease, a fetid, portable commode and the sex-act is a sure sign of degradation:

> Yes, it was ugly, the human figure. Man or woman, it made no difference to Minty. The body's shape, the running nose, excrement, the stupid postures of passion, these beat like a bird's heart in Minty's mind.[36]

There is something abnormal, almost pathological in Minty's revulsion of his own body. He considers it a moral, spiritual coarseness to dress up well, to decorate the body with elegant clothes like Captain Gullie and the British Minister do. Therefore, he remains shabby. The body deserves nothing more than that. When Minty goes to Church, it strikes him as abhorrent that God Himself could have taken on this vile human form.

Pinkie Brown in *Brighton Rock*, is a criminal who reviles the sex-act. This abnormality is the result of his parent's Saturday-night exercise. His witnessing of the primal scene has left him a sexual sadist. His complex is explained in Freudian psychology:

> If children at this early age, witness sexual intercourse between adults—for which an opportunity is provided by the conviction of grown-up people that small children cannot understand anything sexual—they inevitably regard the sexual act as a sort of ill-treatment or an act of subjugation: they view it, that is, in a sadistic sense. Psycho-analysis also shows us that an impression of this kind in early childhood contributes a great deal to a subsequent sadistic displacement of the sexual aim.[37]

Pinkie's relationship to Rose is guided by this same cause. If he gives in to sexual excitement for the moment, it is a sickness to be got over quickly. He reflects that his marriage is a mortal sin. The tragedy is that Rose is committed to his love and resigns herself to his evil designs only to remain unrequited in her desires in the end. The sadistic Pinkie makes her sign the suicide pact. She, in her turn, is ready to go to the other world for his sake. But when Pinkie kills himself, she cannot muster courage to kill herself and is left to endure her loneliness.

For Pinkie, sex is a symbol of the deprivation of parental love in childhood. He concludes that since his parents abandoned him to indulge their passion, all that matters is the self. He hates sex. A view of Rose's thigh disturbs him like a sickness and he thinks of copulation as a dirty scramble that people give fine words to. Love and marriage are anathema to him:

> He didn't want that relationship with anyone; the double bed, the intimacy, it sickened him like the idea of age. . . . To marry—it was like ordure on the hands.[38]

Through the characters of Minty and Pinkie, both described above, Greene is reliving the indoctrinated values of his school-life according to which sex was treated as mortal sin and the human body a dirty vessel.

With Major Scobie in *The Heart of the Matter,* we find that sexual love emanates from pity, but it leads to grave consequences—guilt, damnation and the destruction of the soul. He is a Deputy Commissioner of Police in West Africa. His love contains an element of pride. That is to say, he is proud of his capacity for pity and love. He loves his wife, Louise, and is under a strain to keep up his love for her. Louise is sad because her husband, Scobie has been overlooked for promotion and her ambitions for social status are thwarted. Scobie feels responsible for this failure. His love is also mixed with a pity for her fading youth and age. He is bound to her by the pathos of her unattractiveness. He can keep up the pretence of love because in human relations kindness and lies are worth a thousand truths.[39]

This pretence triggers off a chain of events which carries Scobie to his doom. He gets the finances to send Louise off to South Africa for a holiday. While she is away, he gets embroiled in an adulterous affair. He goes to receive the survivors of a torpedoed ship at a far off border station. One of these is Helen Rolt, a 17 year old girl, clutching an album to herself and with eyes shut. Scobie is overcome with pity for her. He extends his sympathy and commits the act of adultery that is followed by guilt and pricks of conscience:

> Was it the butterfly that died in the act of love? But human beings are condemned to consequences. The responsibility as well as the guilt was his . . . he knew what he was about. He had sworn to preserve Louise's happiness and now he had accepted another contradictory responsibility. He felt tired by all the lies he would sometime have to tell.[40]

Scobie ends up incapable of satisfying either Louise or Helen. Despair is inevitable. He swallows an overdose of Evipan tablets and reaches his end.

The promiscuous love of Maurice Bendrix and Sarah Miles in *The End of the Affair*, reveals all the painful happiness of a short-lived love. Bendrix is a novelist in search of a "copy" for a novel about a civil servant. In the course of his search, he comes across Sarah Miles, wife of a civil servant. The love for her begins casually but soon Bendrix finds himself in the grip of a demonic passion. So great is the passion that he is afraid of losing her and mistrust for Sarah develops. The love gradually develops into hatred and the two become indistinguishable emotions:

> Hatred seems to operate the same glands as love; it even produces the same actions.[41]

Bendrix's love for Sarah has the same element of resignation to a physical necessity or overriding lust. It is nothing more than the emotion of a moment that we find in Pinkie and Andrews, but is much more possessive. I agree with John Atkins' view about the nature of Bendrix's and Sarah's love:

> The grasping, 'coarse,' 'crude,' unaesthetic love of Bendrix and Sarah on a hardwood floor is an adult love. It has managed to discard the notions of romance, pity, morality and equally important, spiritualized psychology. It requires no justification and does not resort to abstraction. It just is.[42]

The passion is instinct with failure. It makes Bendrix jealous and mistrustful of Sarah. The more Sarah gave herself upto him, the more he grew suspicious that she might be lost to someone else or that she might play false with him.

> And yet I could feel no trust in the act of love. I could be arrogant, but alone I had only to look into the mirror to see doubt, in the shape of a lined face and a lame leg—why me?
>
> Distrust grows with a lover's success.[43]

Sarah found Bendrix's love like a medieval chastity belt. She could never assure him of her fidelity. The more she tried, the more it engendered mistrust. Like in Francois Mauriac's characters, the extremes of emotions meet and mingle, becoming indistinguishable in Bendrix:

> I hated her because I wished to think she didn't love me; I wanted to get her out of my system.[44]

Instead of drawing the curtain around the moment of love and enjoying it Bendrix soiled it by a hovering sense of failure.

> But if love had to die, I wanted it to die quickly. It was as though our love were a small creature caught in a trap and

bleeding to death. I had to shut my eyes and wring its neck.[45]

In Greene's love syndrome, the Devil himself is arrayed against any success in love. He seems to plot its destruction by circumstances. Bendrix is knocked off for a moment by a bomb raid. When he recovers, he sees Sarah crouching on the floor on which they used to make love. He imagines she has given herself away to another man. He leaves her for two years. He thinks of suicide but wants to remain alive so that she would not be free from feelings of guilt. This imagination is a demon of suspicion that thwarts every attempt at love:

> I can imagine that if there existed a God who loved, the devil would be driven to destroy even the weakest, the most faulty imitation of that love.[46]

With the help of Parkis, Bendrix gets Sarah's diary. In this he finds that the third lover in the triangle is no other than God. When Bendrix was knocked off during the air-raid, Sarah had prayed to God to allow him to live and to take her own life away instead as a sacrifice for his. She promised to give up her love for Bendrix if this was granted. Her prayer is granted but it means the torment of separation:

> In the shadow of plenitude no quarter is given to the ecstasy of the flesh which must be replaced by the agony of the spirit. Faith brings in its wake, an awful deprivation, the dark night of the soul.[47]

Sarah becomes aware of desolation upon the loss of her love and she finds herself in a desert—the final destiny of Greene lovers.

Reflecting on his creation of Bendrix in his book, *Ways of Escape* (1980), Greene says:

> In *The End of the Affair* I had described a lover who was so afraid that love would end one day, that he tried to hasten the

> end and get the pain over. Yet there was no unhappy love affair to escape this time. I was happy in love. There are difficulties, of course, even in a love affair, but the chief difficulty was my own manic-depressive temperament. So it was that in the fifties I found myself tempting the end to come like Bendrix, but it was the end of life I was seeking, not the end of love.[48]

The same pre-occupation over the years exists—failure in love, failure in life. Greene's sense of failure in life in general, and especially in its chief sustaining emotion, love, germinated in those early brushes with love that ended abortively in adolescence. In the passage above, Greene says that "there was no unhappy love affair to escape this time." But, I think, this is only a temporary phase of life or mind and it is already tinged with sadness, with a foreboding of its evanescent nature. As he says, "There are difficulties, of course, even in a love affair," we sense his reservations about any love being successful. . . . And in the phrase, "the chief difficulty was my own manic-depressive temperament," indicates that this was the manic phase he was undergoing and would as a corollary, swing to the depressive state soon.

In *The Quiet American,* Fowler is haunted by a sense of failure in love with the onus of guilt attached. As in Scobie's case, it springs from a failure of marital life. He is estranged from his wife who lives in England, and being of High Church extraction, she refuses to give him a divorce. His experiences with his wife and other women have given him the truth that human love is fraught with pain. Reading his wife's letter, refusing him a divorce, he reflects:

> Her pain struck at my pain: we were back at the old routine of hurting each other. If only it were possible to love without injury—fidelity isn't enough: I had been faithful to Anne and yet I injured her. The hurt is in the act of possession: we are too small in mind and body to possess another person without pride or to be possessed without humiliation.[49]

Like Bendrix, Fowler is always conscious of the fleeting nature of love and happiness. Only death is a certainty that removes the uncertainty and pain inherent in love:

> Death was far more certain than God and with death there would be no longer the daily possibility of love dying.[50]

Fowler's passion, like Bendrix's, hinged uneasily on the fear of losing his love. There was a girl in a red dressing gown whom he once loved. He

> was terrified of losing her. I thought I saw her changing—I don't know if she really was, but I couldn't bear the uncertainty any longer.[51]

Sex troubles him, but greater is the fear of a lonely old age. He tells Pyle that were he left to the horror of a lonely, old age, he wouldn't know what to think about all day. And if his girl Phuong left him, he wouldn't have the confidence to find another.

As Fowler is unable to offer marriage and settlement to Phuong and his sister, he fears losing them which he does. His middle age cannot match the attraction of Pyle's youth and respectability. And so his love ends in frustration.

Pyle seems to have won Phuong for himself on the grounds of his youth and riches, but Fowler warns him. He has learnt through bitter experience that

> Love's a Western word . . . we use it for sentimental reasons or to cover up an obsession with one woman. These people don't suffer from obsessions. You're going to be hurt, Pyle, if you aren't careful.[52]

Phuong fails to find hope and sincerity from Pyle and falls back on Fowler. Pyle only meets frustration and suffering in trying to arrange Phuong's life according to his own ideas of love and marriage.

In *The Comedians* (1966), Brown begins a casual love-affair with Martha, the South American ambassador's wife. The affair grows into a serious one, with Brown wanting greater proof of Martha's love. Besides, the affair is tinged with the guilt of adultery. They feel like fellow-conspirators in a crime. Like Bendrix in *The End of the Affair,* Brown fears that love might come to an end and this blights his enjoyment of love. Brown's own character acts as a barrier to his trust. Because he was a comedian and believed in role-playing, he thinks Martha must be doing the same. When Jones is in Pineda's Embassy as a refugee, Brown's jealousy makes him imagine that Jones and Martha are playing seducer and mistress. The love affair of Brown and Martha comes to an end by the time they meet in the Dominican Republic. Their parting is as casual as their first meeting. Brown is not a sincere person and is not overcome with frustration by the end of love like in the case of Bendrix and Fowler. He reflects:

> Neither of us would die for love. We would grieve and separate and find another. We belonged to the world of comedy and not of tragedy.[53]

In *The Honorary Consul,* Plarr forfeits his love in the game of rivalry with Charley Fortnum, just like in *The Quiet American,* Fowler loses his love to Pyle. Plarr's love for Clara begins casually and clumsily. Clara is an ex-whore from Senora Sanchez's brothel. She is an unattractive, immature, child-like woman. Plarr only wonders whether it is rational to love her, yet he becomes obsessed and takes her to bed. But the act of love brings in its wake depression. Lust is replaced by tender feelings for Clara. Plarr is jealous of Fortnum's love for Clara and he tells Aquino:

> I am jealous because he loves her. That stupid banal word love. It's never meant anything to me. Like the word God. I know how to fuck—I don't know how to love. Poor drunken Charley Fortnum wins the game.[54]

The theme of pity and love leading to tragic consequences which was developed in *The Heart of the Matter,* which I have already discussed earlier in this chapter, resurfaced with Myatt and Coral Musker in *Stamboul Train.* On her way to Constantinople to participate in a troupe programme, Coral Musker realizes that life is ugly and brutal. In the railway compartment, she faints in the corridor from cold and hunger. Carleton Myatt, a young Jew thrown on himself by the hatred of the world and conscious of his wealth is stirred to pity for her. Of course, his sexual instincts are also aroused and he gives up his first class sleeper to her. Grateful for this, Coral gives herself up to Myatt and she longs now for a better life as Myatt's mistress:

> Away from the rattling metal, the beating piston, she stepped in thought, wrapping a fur coat round her, up the stairs to her flat... she laughed out and clapped her hands with the sudden sense that love was a simple affair made up of gratitude and gifts and familiar jokes, a flat, no work and a maid.[55]

But in Greene, love is stalked by a cruel destiny which turns happiness into a nightmare. The ironical pessimism of Thomas Hardy and A.E. Housman informs Greene's attitude to love. Coral is swept away by a chain of events to her tragic end. She is arrested at Subotica along with Czinner. Czinner is a communist, and after spending five years in exile as a school teacher in England, is returning to Belgrade to lead a communist uprising when he is arrested. Myatt is not in the compartment when she is arrested. The soldier who arrests her cannot understand what she says. Czinner is hit by a bullet and Coral feels she cannot leave the wounded man alone. And so she remains to help him and is caught by the soldier.

Raven, the mercenary killer in *A Gun for Sale* is destined from birth for betrayal. Life has never been kind to him. Born with an ugly harelip, he is loved by no one. And the only time he does trust someone, his betrayal leads to his capture. He saves a girl called Anne at the risk of his own life. He feels a passionate desire to confess his secrets because he had never been able to confide in anyone yet. He tells her about his past—his mother's suicide, Kite's murder and the great revelation—the assassination of the minister which lies like an Albatross around his neck. Anne is simply horrified to learn of this last fact, but promises to keep her mouth shut. But as soon as she meets her fiance, Detective Sergeant Mather, she betrays Raven. Raven learns of his coup de grace to his unhappy life. His already tiny faith in man is extinguished before his death:

> He had been marked from his birth for this end.... How could he have expected to have escaped the commonest betrayal of all, to go soft on a skirt?[56]

In *The Human Factor,* the theme is failure of marital life as in *The Quiet American,* which I have treated earlier in this chapter. In *The Human Factor,* Daintry lives estranged from his wife and daughter. A sense of guilt descends on him for the failure of his marriage as he meets his daughter in a public place:

> It was odd to think there had ever been a time when he and his wife were close enough to share a sexual spasm which had produced the beautiful girl who sat so elegantly opposite him drinking her Tio Pepe. The sadness which was never far away from Daintry when he met his daughter descended as always like a sense of guilt. Why guilt? After all she had consented to marry him knowing all; she had voluntarily entered that chilling world of long silences.[57]

In the same book, *The Human Factor,* Castle is an unhappy agent of police, with a sense of inadequacy about his power to love his wife. The germ of this failure to love satisfactorily lies in an experience of sexual suffering in childhood. One day he nostalgically visits the scene of his childhood love. Fifty years ago, he had discovered a hollow in the trunk of one of the trees there. He was then ten, and he had left a message in the hollow of the tree for a girl he loved. She was only seven. He had told her that the next time he came he would leave something important for her in it. His visit now at 60, floods him with associations:

> In those days he had been forced to stretch almost his full height to reach the hole, but his heart had knocked in the same erratic fashion as it did now.[58]

On the first occasion, Castle had left a large peppermint humbug wrapped in grease proof paper, and when he came back to the hole, it had gone. Then he left a letter there saying he loved her. He wrote it in capitals because she had just learnt to read. When he returned he found the letter still there, but with a vulgar drawing on it. Some stranger might have found the hiding place, he thought. But he saw her on the High Street and she put her tongue out at him, and hc realized she was disappointed because he had not put another humbug there. "It had been his first experience of sexual suffering. . . ."[59]

This story of Castle reminds one of Greene's short stories written earlier, "The Innocent," written in 1937. A man takes a tart back to his childhood hometown for the night. He is overcome by nostalgia, the smell of innocence. He slips out to look at a house where he had dancing lessons. He had once loved a little girl there, but she had taken no notice of him. It was childhood love unrequited. He remembered how he had left messages filled with a beautiful passion for her in a hole in the gatepost (similar to the hollow in the tree-trunk that Castle used). One was still there when the man returned after years. He took it out to read the beautiful passion, but there was, instead, an obscene drawing in it. The drawing was his own. But it had seemed so innocent when he drew it as a child.

"Frustration in Love" is the recurrent theme of Greene's novels reminiscent of his own experiences in childhood. Various reasons contrive to frustrate love from reaching fulfilment. With Andrews, lust for Lucy deprives him of his pure love for Elizabeth; with Drover adultery is the tragic flaw; Scobie is led away to his doom by the sense of pity. Bendrix is soured by doubts and mistrust;

Pinkie and Minty have a pathological abhorrence for sex; Fowler and Plarr lose in the game of sexual rivalry; Raven is betrayed by feminine friskiness; Coral Musker is snatched away by cruel destiny and Castle suffers from a sense of sexual disappointment since childhood.

That first frustration of calf-love at 17, which Greene describes in his autobiography is a foreboding of all the failed human relationships of his novels. David Pryce Jones aptly summarizes the recurrent pattern traced by the love-affairs of Greene's anti-heroes:

> It is as if Greene saw a line stretching from birth to death with a time scale on it and an innocence-meter attached. Each friendship or love will bring the arrow on the indicator a little nearer death and corruption, for this is the nature of human existence. Time will bring love, love will being betrayal, betrayal will bring corruption. The more the scales are interfered with, the faster will the indicator swing downward.[60]

NOTES

1. Greene, Graham, *England Made Me,* Heinemann, London, (Uniform ed), 1955, p. 60.
2. Atkins, John, *Graham Greene,* Calder Boyars, London, 1957, p. 46.
3. Greene, Graham, *A Sort of Life,* Penguin, London, 1971, p. 11.
4. Ibid., p. 58.
5. Ibid., p. 59.
6. Ibid., p. 58.
7. Ibid., p. 67.
8. Greene, Graham (ed.) *The Old School,* Cape, London, 1934, p. 17.
9. Atkins, John, p. 48.

10. Freud, Sigmund, *Three Theories of Sexuality,* Avon, New York, 1962, p. 94.
11. Ibid., p. 73.
12. Greene, Graham, *A Sort of Life,* p. 31.
13. Ibid., pp. 42-43.
14. Ibid., p. 44.
15. Greene, Graham, "The End of the Party," in *Perspectives,* S.A. Vasudevan & M. Sathya Babu, Macmillan, Delhi, p. 142.
16. Greene, Graham, *England Made Me,* p. 67.
17. Greene, Graham, *A Sort of Life,* pp. 55-56.
18. Ibid., p. 84.
19. Ibid., pp. 84-85.
20. Ibid., p. 86.
21. Russell, Bertrand, *Why I am Not a Christian,* Simon and Schuster, New York, 1957, p. 82.
22. Isherwood, Christopher, "Lions and Shadows," quoted in Bernard Bengonzi's *Reading the Thirties,* Macmillan, London and Basingstoke, 1979, p. 11.
23. Ibid., p. 13.
24. Greene, Graham, *A Sort of Life,* p. 87.
25. Ibid., p. 132.
26. Ibid., p. 173.
27. Greene, Graham, "1930" in *Babbling April,* Oxford, Basil Blackwell, 1925, p. 16.
28. Greene, Graham, *The Man Within,* Heinemann, London, 1927, p. 209.
29. Ibid., pp. 128-129.
30. Greene, Graham, *A Sort of Life,* p. 15.
31. Greene, Graham, *It's a Battlefield,* Heinemann, London (Uniform ed.), 1956, p. 144.
32. Ibid., p. 204.
33. Ibid., p. 197.
34. Greene, Graham, *England Made Me,* p. 258.
35. Ibid., p. 150.
36. Ibid., p. 109.

37. Freud, Sigmund, *Three Theories of Sexuality*, p. 94.
38. Greene, Graham, *Brighton Rock*, Heinemann, London, (Uniform Ed.), 1955, p. 132.
39. Greene, Graham, *The Heart of the Matter*, The Reprint Society, London, 1950, p. 69.
40. Ibid., p. 171.
41. Greene, Graham, *The End of the Affair*, Heinemann, London, (Library Ed.), 1959, pp. 26-27.
42. Atkins, John, *Graham Greene*, p. 20.
43. Greene, Graham, *The End of the Affair*, p. 53.
44. Ibid., p. 63.
45. Ibid., p. 37.
46. Ibid., p. 68.
47. Ibid., p. 121.
48. Greene, Graham, *Ways of Escape*, The Bodley Head, London, 1980, pp. 139-140.
49. Greene, Graham, *The Quiet American*, Heinemann, London (Uniform Ed.), 1960, pp. 152-53.
50. Ibid., pp. 49-50.
51. Ibid., p. 131.
52. Ibid., p. 172.
53. Greene, Graham, *The Comedians*, The Bodley Head, London, 1966, p. 176.
54. Greene, Graham, *The Honorary Consul*, Penguin Books, London, 1964, p. 251.
55. Greene, Graham, *Stamboul Train*, Heinemann, London (Library Ed.), 1959, pp. 124-125.
56. Greene, Graham, *A Gun for Sale*, Heinemann, London, p. 221.
57. Greene, Graham, *The Human Factor*, The Bodley Head, London, 1980, p. 106.
58. Ibid., pp. 185-86.
59. Ibid.
60. Pryce-Jones, David, *Graham Greene*, Oliver Boyd, London, p. 20.

Failure-Fixation

> *. . . one looked around and saw the doomed everywhere—the champion runner who one day would sag over the tape; . . . and when success began to touch oneself too, however mildly, one could only pray that failure would not be held off for too long.*[1]

This passage from his autobiography shows that in childhood at school Greene realized that failure was inherent in success. Failure lurked in all the great plans of man. This instinctive realization was the prelude to Greene's failure-fixation.

Yet the paradox is that Graham Greene is, today, one of the world's most successful writers in English with more than thirty works translated into twenty-one languages to his credit. His novels have proved uniquely cinematic and all have been turned into films. A plethora of critical literature has been written on his works and if money is any criterion for success, he is certainly well-off. Now, even at eighty-five he leads an active life which a prosperous man can afford. He travels to South America, Switzerland and England. He keeps a flat in Paris. and a house in Capri, but lives nowadays in the Antibes in France. Says Radek Sikiorski, reporting an interview with Greene for *The Sunday Statesman:*

> He is almost certainly the best-selling English author ever.[2]

Awards and acclaim have come to him from many directions. In 1966, he was made a Companion of Honour and in 1984 he was bestowed the Companion of Literature. In fact, Greene's fans have wondered why he has not been considered for the great Nobel Prize yet. Greene himself has a generous reason for this:

> I'm too old. Also I have a deadly enemy on the committee called Arthur Lundquist . . . and he said it would be 'over his dead body'. I don't even know whether I ever met the man. . . . But it may be political. He is a Lenin Prize winner. Another reason they say is, that I don't need the money and I don't. I have quite a lot of people to support, but . . . I'm not poor.[3]

On the eve of his eightieth birthday, *The Sunday Statesmen* of September 30, 1984, published views on Greene from various eminent people in responsible public posts. They have lauded different aspects of his creative works. The novelist, Angus Wilson eulogizes the profundity of Greene's thinking:

> It was 1938. A time when we all needed painful truths that would stick. Did not want easy answers that would fade after they had jogged us along a little. We all needed a confirmation of the forces that were manifesting themselves. Needed to realize, and more important to feel, something deeper than just right or wrong, good guys and rotten eggs. . . . Ida it was, I think, that first gave me the sense that Graham Greene's novels had a depth that was unknown to the novel of that day which was also a good story.[4]

Greene's religious views have struck many Catholics and moralists as either curious, or shocking, yet he has universal appeal. A.J. Ayer, philosopher and author, throws light on this point:

> I admire the works of Graham Greene more than those of any other living novelist. This is in spite of the fact that I wholly lack the religious faith which inspires some of his best books like 'The Heart of the Matter' and 'The Power and the Glory'. . . . It is encouraging to note how successful he has been in maintaining his standards throughout his eight decades. 'The

Human Factor' which appeared in 1978, was as moving as anything that he has written.[5]

His non-conformist stance in matters of dogma, show him up as original and he is often admired for being an iconoclast, turning traditional views in religion and ethics inside out and for making us rethink our ideas all over again. The famous writer, Malcolm Muggeridge apprises Greene thus:

> The prospect of becoming the G.O.M. of English Letters would at one time have appalled Graham Greene. Now, on his eightieth birthday, it must be seen as a just recognition of a long and variegated life dedicated to the craft of writing. . . . He is, indeed, the most skillful and conscientious of contemporary writers.
>
> Then—what has always fascinated men—there is his Catholicism, which, despite heresies and irregularities, has continued to occupy his mind and perhaps also his soul. I cherish the memory of walking up and down with him by the Sea of Galilee and talking about the Incarnation as expounded in the New Testament. His favourite text is also mine: 'Lord I believe; help thou mine unbelief.'[6]

Amalendu Das Gupta commends Greene's plot-making skill as breath-taking. "Some speak of his deadly accuracy of phrase."[7]

Greene, it is true, has had his detractors. For example, John Atkins accuses Greene's hollow theology:

> Greene's theology, when stripped of the skill with which it is presented, is really little more than a complicated metaphorical structure. There are terrifying moments when one feels it exists merely to ward off the truth.[8]

Yet the criticism on Greene is so weighted on the side of his being an all-round success, that faults like the above-mentioned by Atkins fade into mere peccadilloes. The overwhelming fact established in 1989 in that he is one of the most successful writers in English. But the great paradox is that Greene has suffered from an unmistakable failure-fixaton since childhood. As a schoolboy, he thought he would never succeed in making meaning of life and attempted suicide. His first literary works, poetry and novels were either abandoned prematurely or never got to the publishers. The characters of all his anti-heroes in his successful novels are failures in their particular vocation in life, or when they seem to be apparently successful in their profession, failure gnaws them in other respects. In their moral and spiritual self-analysis, they are burdened with an extreme sense of failure that reduces their worldly success to nought. Even at the time in childhood when Greene received credit for a work, like his first story "The Tick of the Clock," the temporary excitement was followed by a hovering sense of failure. This piece about the death of a solitary old woman was published in his school (St. John's) magazine. It was also accepted by a paper called `The Star' which paid him three guineas for it. He read the editor's letter to himself a number of times on an abandoned rifle-butts in Berkhamstead Common. This was the first and last time that a feeling of success touched him. He writes:

> Always later, even with the publication of my first novel, the excitement was overshadowed by the knowledge of failure, by awareness of the flawed intention.[9]

This "awareness of the flawed intention" as Greene puts it is a steady theme in his life from childhood to present times. Now, when accolades are being showered on him for being a great writer, he is hesitant about accepting the fact without reservations. He said in an interview:

> I think I'm not a bad writer, which is a form of success, but one is never the writer one would like to have been. One would like to have been able to be mentioned with the truly great, who all seem to belong to the 19th century.[10]

Besides showing Greene's modesty and acceptance of human limitations the statement above is tinged with reservation about full success. For all Greene's reservation, he was in Atkins' words "doomed to succeed."[11]

What are the origins of Greene's failure-consciousness which doom his characters? They must lie in childhood experiences. It is not possible to state exactly where the origin of such an attitude lay or when and how it developed. But, one can guess strongly by referring to Greene's own confessions in his autobiography, *A Sort of Life*. Failure broods over the autobiography from beginning to end. It begins on a pessimistic notc:

> An autobiography is only 'a sort of life'—it may contain less errors of fact than a biography, but it is of necessity even more selective; it begins later and it ends prematurely. If one cannot close a book of memories on the death bed, any conclusion must be arbitrary, and I have preferred to finish this essay with the acceptance of my first novel. Failure too is a kind of death: the furniture sold, the drawers emptied, the removal van waiting like a hearse in the lane to take one to a less expensive destination.[12]

John Atkins tries to trace Greene's sense of failure to certain events in early childhood that must have left deep psychological and spiritual scars on the impressionable mind:

> His obsession with failure could take a neurotic shape. . . . He said failure hadn't the shamelessness of success; 'it might be vulgar, but it wasn't successfully vulgar.' But that wasn't the reason, and I doubt if he would press it now. We would have to trace it to some stupendous event in his past, such as an attempt at suicide, or the pretence of such an attempt, followed by remorse—and I will consider the possibility later. All I can do at this stage is state, and reiterate, the fact of

> Greene's inner contradiction, like two live charges crossing each other—perhaps evidence of a personal version of Newman's 'aboriginal catastrophe' which may very well have prepared Greene for his religious conversion. Perhaps it was precipitated by his first memory of a dead dog, at the bottom of his pram. It had been run over and his nurse had picked it up and put it in. There was no emotion attached to the sight. Then there was the man who rushed out of a cottage with a knife in his hand, threatening to kill himself.[13]

Besides the scenes of death that must have conveyed the sense of "aboriginal catastrophe" and of the failure of finding meaning in life, Greene had to face failure with his earliest literary attempts. These setbacks must have dampened his enthusiasm and haunted him in his professional career. On his return from the psycho-analysis at Richmond's, he bagan to write sentimental fantasies in bad poetic prose. One piece called "The Tick of the Clock," already mentioned, was the only one successful. It was to be followed with failures in his other works. In his autobiography, *A Sort of Life,* Greene describes his attempt at a fantastic play, the title of which he forgot later on. He had been influenced by Maurice Hewlett and Dunsany's "Lost Silk Hat." This play

> celebrated the ceremony of afternoon tea with its lavish aesthetic touches.[14]

He sent it to a dramatic society in 1920 (he was 15 years old then) and was hoping excitedly for a letter accepting the play for production. He went up to London to meet the management. But there was an overblown, rosy woman there who was astonished to see him as she realized that he was only a schoolboy, not a "rich sucker,"[15] who could finance the play and help her foot her domestic bills.

At this time, Greene began to have dreams of wishfulfilment. His desires and fears surfaced in dreams for twenty years. He dreamt he was an established writer making enough money. Greene wrote a volume of verse "which is now an expensive curiosity for collectors."[16] Greene's first novel written at Oxford was about his first and last great pre-occupation—childhood and unhappiness. Greene recalls:

> The first chapter described the hero's birth in an old country house. It seemed to me at the time a piece of rich, evocative writing, and so it tried to be, but of the Jacobean rhythms of Walter de La Mare's prose rather than of personal experience. . . . There followed in my novel a hushed up childhood and a lonely colour-barred life at school, but to me even then the end seemed badly botched.[17]

Failure stalked his second and third novels, too. These were entitled, *The Name of Action* and *Rumour at Nightfall* and were published respectively in 1930 and 1931. They were suppressed after their first publication by Greene. Greene has left strict orders in his will that they should never be published in extract or any other form. He has also condemned the novels for their quality:

> They can be found, I am glad to think, only in second-hand bookshops at an exaggerated price, since some years after their publication I suppressed them. Both books are of a badness beyond the power of criticism to properly evoke—the prose flat and stilted and in the case of *Rumour at Nightfall* pretentious.[18]

The fear of failure stalks him with each new book. In fact, fear makes him superstitious. Is Greene only being humorous when he writes:

> Perhaps all writers are superstitious. The hero of *The Name of Action* was called Chant, the two protagonists of *Rumour at Nightfall* were Chase and Crane. The books were failures and failure seemed to cling around the letter C. I abandoned C. I thought for ever, and a sense of doom descended on me when

> I named the chief character in "The Human Factor," Castle. I tried my best to give him another name, but there is a magic quality in a name—to change the name is to change the character. Castle it had to be, but I went ahead with a sense of almost certain failure.[19]

About his third novel, Greene says:

> it was the last throw of the dice in a game I had practically lost.[20]

The two previous novels had been refused by every publisher approached. So Greene had determined to give up the ambition of becoming a writer, if the third failed too. He would "settle down to the safe and regular life of a sub editor in Room2 of 'The Times.'"[21]

Although the acceptance and publication of *The Man Within* settled his decision in favour of the career of a writer, Greene has his reservations about the diction of this novel. About the opening line of the novel itself, he says:

> It is not a good line, for it has the ring of verse rather than prose.[22]

The theme of failure is recurrent in his novels. His characters are obsessed with failure like Greene himself. The following characters may be considered here:

1. Anthony Farrant of *England Made Me*.
2. The Assistant Commissioner in *It's a Battlefield*.
3. The Priest in *The Power and the Glory*.
4. Dr. Czinner in *Stamboul Train*.
5. Querry in *A Burnt-Out Case*.
6. Thomas Fowler in *The Quiet American*.
7. Brown and Jones in *The Comedians*.
8. Dr. Eduardo Plarr and Leon Rivas in *The Honorary Con-*

sul.

9. Castle in *The Human Factor.*
10. Dr. Benjamin Jowett in *The Great Jowett.*

The characters do not appear in order of the year of their creation (that is, the publication of the books). They are depicted as having failed to live normal, successful lives as human beings because of childhood traumas, e.g., Pinkie, Raven, Drover, Rowe etc. I have taken failure here to mean failure in their professional fields or failure to measure up to full moral and spiritual health despite worldly success.

Anthony Farrant and Minty are English declasses, the jetsam and flotsam of a moribund society. Anthony sees Minty and himself as the same person:

> the exile from his country and his class, the tramp whose workhouses were Shanghai, Aden, Singapore, the refuse of a changing world.[23]

Anthony reappears as the character Hands, the hero of Greene's abandoned novel, *The Other Side of the Border.* Both Anthony and Hands thrive on lies, borrowed money and accumulated failures. At the age of thirty-three, Anthony has had pot-shots at different jobs and now bears the "knobs, excrescences and fungi of a dozen careers."[24] He signifies for his sister, Kate, disgrace, and everything except success. He is conceited with failure, has no future and covers his counterfeit self with elegance and false bonhomie. He wears a Harrovian tie he is not entitled to. The English girl from Coventry, Loo (Lucia Devidge) who is his partner for weaker moments of the flesh, tells him that his job as the millionaire Krogh's bodyguard is not respectable. This fact only feeds his self-estimate. He discovers Krogh's shady business deals, and his penchant for deception goads him to exploit Krogh by blackmailing him. His foolhardy innocence is the key to his failure. He only arouses Krogh's suspicions about his further reliability. Anthony knows too much to be safe enough to live. So he is pushed into a lake and drowned by Hall, Krogh's devoted mastiff-in-waiting. Anthony's death is an inevitable corollary of a long drawn-out failure which imposed a bias on his life and aggravated his vulnerability.

Anthony is a projection of Greene's sense of failure. In fact, he is Greene's alter ego. Erik Krogh of *England Made Me* is the owner of a vast industrial empire. His financial credit stands at a point higher than that of the French government. His initials speak to him from various parts of his office building and are like

> the lights of a semaphore conveying a message over the vast distances which separated him from other men.[25]

But, in Greene's world, this materialistic success is just another great failure. Krogh is doomed to alienation and loneliness. The greater he has acquired wealth, the more have his values become dehumanised. All human relationships are considered in terms of money. In the Opera he sits in a small wilderness of his own contriving, an empty seat on either hand. He has risen from humble origins and he realizes that his past was happy despite its poverty. At least he had the warmth of human company. His oldest friend, Hall now works for him and calls him very formally "Mr. Krogh." In the baneful drive to become richer and richer all human values are thrown overboard. Lies, deception, murder of people working for him are all within the game. He has Anthony, who was loyal to him, murdered because Anthony knows his secrets and is leaving with them. David Pryce-Jones observes that

> Krogh is as much a prisoner of his fortune as the others are the victims of their poverty. Krogh's freedom is of the same order as Minty; both the mental vagrants.[26]

Minty, who is a seedy reporter or journalist of Krogh's activities finds his own seediness and failure in Krogh:

> He's only one of us. He has no more roots than we have.[27]

Kate also realizes the same:

> He's one of us, fighting for his own security like one of us, he's not the future, he's not self-sufficient, just one of us, out of his proper place.[28]

Scobie, in *The Heart of the Matter*, like many forerunners, loves failure. The differences between him and Anthony is that it is unforgivable in his metier. At least, no one expects Anthony to succeed. When Scobie was passed over for promotion, it was his wife who suffered and not he. And similarly, when the decision was reversed and he was promoted to Police Commissioner it was his wife who was filled with a desire to live for she was overjoyed. Scobie found himself hating her for her complacency. Her adult innocence is nauseating. He rationalized that even God was a failure and it enabled him to love God. Just before committing suicide, he was overcome with love for Louise again because he knew that her social triumph was really a failure. It could not last long. Nothing lasted. Not even beauty and it was failure that Scobie loved. This is one of Greene's common inventions of values. David Pryce Jones explains this equation of anomalies:

> Success makes people love themselves, people loving themselves do not love God, therefore failure is beloved of God, and the nearest approximation to love of God. This too allows word-play, for Christ failing to save Himself from death is a magnificent success. This is as essential to Greene as the pseudo syllogism built around love and lust, and love and passion. It explains . . . Scobie's suicide, for 'by knowing the worst' in Scobie's words, they are humans as God intended them to be when He made them. Success is the artificial acquisition of worldly trappings which will keep the camel away from the eye of the needle.[29]

The Assistant Commissioner in *It's a Battlefield* by virtue of his training and the nature of his job as the head of the police eschelon, has to maintain a disinterested distance from all people in London and from his subordinates. This means loneliness and mistrust from everyone around him and he is left either in his apartment or in his office like a general surveying reports coming in from different departments. He has only old age and retirement to look forward to. The only thing of value he can cling on to tenaciously is his devotion to his job. It is

> the only thing it was certainly right to do, the only human value valid for every change of Government, and for every change of heart.[30]

However, a sense of obvious futility informs his loyalty to his profession. He seems to be just holding on to it for want of any meaning in life, but he is only too conscious of its not working perfectly. He knows he is avowed to a cause that does not always have justification. He has no belief in the validity of the system he serves or in the rightness of his actions.

> In the case of Drover he was upholding a system in which he had no interest . . . he was a mercenary. . . . He fought because he was paid to fight, and only occasionally did the sight of some brutality lend conviction to the brain with which he fought.[31]

He would like to serve a cause which was valid by its justness and reasonableness. But it is impossible for him to achieve this great directing purpose in a world of suffering and injustice. When he hears of Jim Drover's reprieve and Conrad Drover's death (the opposites of which he was fighting for), he feels half-inclined to resign.

The Priest in *The Power and the Glory,* may have found God and been martyred towards the end of a spiritual struggle and repentance, but ostensibly, in his vocation as a priest, as a man, he is one of Greene's greatest failures. He is a bad priest and is haunted by his failure and corruption. One of his dreams reveals he was never a very devout priest. In his Concepcion days, he was surrounded by the corrupting influences of life—great dinners and honours and he was proud and complacent. Now he has become a whiskey priest, proud, lustful and greedy, loving the spoils of the earth. His sinful life has degraded him in the eyes of his people and God. He has failed in a series of priestly vows and has played into the hands of the Devil. He drinks and has sired a child, Brigitta who is horribly mature and the corruption of the world is already in her. He loves her and in this way loves his sin and therefore cannot bring himself to repentance:

> That was true: he had lost the faculty. He couldn't say to himself that he wished his sin had never existed, because the sin seemed to him now so important—and he loved the fruit of it.[32]

Just before the execution, a poignant nostalgia takes his mind back to ambitions, cherished in childhood. His life, his vocation had been a failure to achieve his goals:

> It had been a happy childhood, except that he had been afraid of too many things, and hated poverty like a crime: he had believed he would be rich and proud—that was called having a vocation. He thought of the immeasurable distance a man travels—from the first whipping-top to this bed, on which he lay clasping the brandy. And to God it was only a moment. The child's snigger and the first mortal sin lay together more closely than two blinks of the eye.[33]

He cannot redeem himself, he feels, and his damnation is certain. "Evil runs like malaria in his veins."[34] He miserably clings on to his faith in God and despite his overwhelming sense of failure performs his duties, never hopeful of salvation. He admits to a fellow prisoner in the prison cell that he is a bad priest. At the time when awaiting his execution, he makes his private confession (sacramental confession was not permitted to him) and is acutely conscious of having failed:

> I have done nothing for anyone, I might just as well have never lived. Tears poured down his face, he was not at the moment afraid of damnation—even the fear of pain was in the background. He felt an immense disappointment because he had to go to God empty-handed, with nothing done at all. . . . He felt like someone who has missed happiness by seconds at an appointed place.[35]

The tragic case of Dr. Czinner in *Stamboul Train,* further shows Greene's belief in failure. Dr. Czinner was born and brought up in the slums of Belgrade and was a staunch Socialist. He believed in an ideal for the world based on Communism:

> The wealth of the world belonged to everyone. If it was divided, there would be no rich men, but every man would have enough to eat, and would have no reason to feel ashamed beside his neighbour.[36]

But his dreams are going to come to nought. He has spent five years in exile as a school teacher in England and is going back to Belgrade to lead a Communist Uprising. He is a weary, lonely man, bitterly conscious of having failed his parents, his cause to the poor and to God. In the train he clings to the loneliness of the compartment. Introspection shows him that he has failed himself as a Socialist. He is travelling First Class in the train though his people belonged to the third. He had given his evidence at the Kamnetz trial in vain and now is on his way to rejoin his people to reaffirm his solidarity with them but is intercepted by his arrest at Subotica. He learns that he has been betrayed by his own people who started the communist uprising three days too early and dashed his hopes to nothing.

> They had ruined him with them. They had left him in an empty house which could not find a tenant because old ghosts were

sometimes vocal in the rooms, and Dr. Czinner now was not even the latest ghost.[37]

Dr. Czinner gets no trial in Belgrade and there is no one to listen to him or rise for him. He dies a victim of political violence.

Querry of *A Burn-out Case* (1961) is a successful architect. Yet he is gnawed by a sense of vacuity, of emptiness which is really spiritual. He feels the weariness of success which has proved inane and has left him with only unhappiness. He realizes that like the leper in the leprosorie he is 'a burnt-out case.' That is to say, just as the disease has run its full course in the leper and has reduced his fingers and toes to stubs, so has Querry reached a state of utter futility. He realizes that whatever he has done till now, all his work as an artist or a lover has been for love of self and nothing positive remains in his heart. His worldly success has achieved nothing for anyone and he is unhappily successful. He brings this fact out in a story he tells Marie Rycker at a hotel at Luc. A jeweller had made beautiful jewels in honour of a king whose existence he merely postulated by philosophical and historical logic. But he found out that the king never existed and that his work and success were useless. They had only made him heartless with pride. The parable is the story of Querry himself, and we may surmise, of Greene himself, who found worldly success a type of failure, of a happy life).

> It needs a very strong vocation to withstand success. The popular priest and the popular architect—their talents can be killed easily by disgust.[38]

Querry has come to Africa, to a leperosorie in the Congo, to run away from the glamour of wordly success. He feels that in Africa, man is preserved from the tortures of civilisation. People live in a state of consciousness before thought and rationalization, and therefore they are always happy, singing and dancing. This state is called Pendele (a word Querry gets from his servant Deo Gratias). Querry feels that he would be able to regain his passiön for living, his freedom from mental and spiritual aridity here in Africa. But the world catches up with Querry and swamps his attempts to find his freedom from worldly success. Father Thomas sees in his spiritual self-analysis and aridity the dark night of the soul that precedes sainthood. A certain Rycker (the manager of a factory), sees Querry as a way to answering his spiritual problems and latches himself on to Querry, and Parkinson, the journalist arrives on his trail to do a write-up on the famous man. Parkinson wants to create Querry as "An Architect of Souls," "The Hermit of the Congo" through his pen. Mrs. Rycker provokes his pity and love with her unhappiness. All of them destroy his dream of "Pendele" by involving him emotionally. He is shot by Rycker who suspects him of an illegitimate love affair with Mrs. Rycker. His success has proved his greatest failure.

Querry feels 'an extraordinary weariness.' He is being caught up in the trammels of the world from which he thought he had escaped. The dream for Pendele is finally shattered, ironically enough, when Querry learns to feel compassion for human suffering and realizes the necessity of involvement. Querry has victimised women all his life and now he is victimized by one of them.

Thomas Fowler the journalist who narrates the story in *The Quiet American* shows again Greene's preoccupation with flawed human beings. Fowler cannot find meaning or interest in life. Since he cannot bear the inhuman cruelties of the American war in Vietnam (he is deeply moved on seeing an innocent mother and a child killed in the line), he gives up and will not have himself involved or committed to any cause. This is the result of his frustration. Like Conrad's character Axel Heyst, he realizes that any type of participation only leads to evil in life and therefore, he has withdrawn himself into a cocoon of impersonal observation. In fact it is a type of futility in the face of people's horrible commitment. He cannot understand the dangerous innocence of Alden Pyle whose idealism of "isms" and "cracies" is only causing the death of innocents in Vietman. Fowler's decisiveness is finally scotched by a paralysed will. He says:

> It had been an article of my creed. The human condition being what it was, let them fight, let them love, let them murder, I would not be involved.[39]

Fowler realizes his wretched failure and he is filled with self-pity. He is a picture of seediness:

> a man of middle age, with eyes a little bloodshot, beginning to put on weight, ungraceful in love, less noisy than Granger (an American reporter) perhaps, but more cynical, less innocent.[40]

An exile who has lived in Saigon almost friendless, he smokes opium and shirks work. He enjoys teasing others like Pyle. He admits that his cynicism is only a weapon of weakness.

Fowler has despaired of all belief and faith. He has ended up as an agnostic.

> Perhaps that's why men have invented God—a being capable of understanding. Perhaps if I wanted to be understood or to understand I would bamboozle myself into belief, but I am a reporter; God exists only for leader-writers.[41]

Fowler's only means of freedom from the anxieties and fears of life is death. He yearns for death and welcomes it during a gunfire, although he is afraid of it. Death is the only absolute value on earth.

> Lose life and one would lose nothing for ever. Death was far more certain than God. . . .[42]

Fowler's life is, indeed the story of failure of an individual to find meaning in a horrifying existence which has led to utter despair and complete loss of faith in any redeeming power.

Brown and Jones are *The Comedians* (published in 1966), whose failure stems from two causes. One, they are both rootless, being migrants to Haiti. Two, like Fowler they are uncommitted to any cause like communism etc.

Brown owns Hotel Trianon at Port-an-Prince. Unable to sell his hotel to someone in the United States, he is returning to Haiti where he has only fear and frustration waiting for him. He has no roots anywhere. He cannot call Haiti his home, either, because it is a land of terror. He was born in Monaco of a British father and a mother of dubious nationality.

Like Fowler in *The Quiet American* Brown Lacks any power of involvement. He was educated by Catholic Jesuits and might have had belief once which is now destroyed by a life in which one role-playing has succeeded another. His Jesuit training has given him a conscience which nags his sense of responsibility and he envies people like Doctor Magiot the Communist, who have some belief. But experiences have left him incapable of commitment to any cause. He says:

> I should never have come to this country, I was a stranger. My mother had taken a black lover, she had been involved, but somewhere years ago I had forgotten how to be involved in anything.[43]

Brown's failure to act in a world of evil which demands commitment, leaves him with a sense of having failed in life. However, his rootlessness and incapacity to succeed in life, to make sense out of it has not altogether killed his faith, like in the case of Fowler. Brown reflects:

> When I was boy I had faith in the Christian God. Life under his shadow was a very serious affair; I saw Him incarnated in every tragedy.... Now that I approached the end of life it was only my sense of humour that enabled me sometimes to believe in Him.[44]

He does not think too deeply about the ultimate truth of things and he is buoyed up a little by his playing the role of a comedian. But his humour only salves his consciousness of failure in the face of reality.

In the same novel, *The Comedians,* the character called Jones has all the makings of a fraud. He has made his way through life with suave lies and tall talk like Anthony Farrant in *England Made Me.* He lies that he is a Major to pass off as respectable. Like Anthony, he knows how to make friends, and plays different roles. He has got along like this in various parts of the world like Burma and the Congo, and comes to Haiti with his phoney credentials. At heart he is innocent like Anthony in a world of corruption. He impresses the Haitian government with his lies and makes the insurgents believe in his skill as a commando leader who could train them in guerilla warfare. The Haitian government discovers his fraudulence and he has to seek asylum in the South American embassy. Dr. Magiot exploits Jones' desire to boast in front of Martha. Dr. Magiot wants him out of the embassy to train the insurgents. He dies in a rearguard action. Jones real personality is always covered in a mask of role-playing which he sheds when confessing his lies and dissimulations. He is a study of a human being who fails to win anything by playing his own character and whose innocent mask proves his undoing anyway.

Dr. Eduardo Plarr of *The Honorary Consul* (1964) has failed to find fulfilment and meaning in human existence, being rootless like Dr. Czinner, Brown and Jones and Fowler, the characters already described. A young man in his thirties, Dr. Plarr is the son of an English father and a Paraguayan mother. His father, a political activist, is either dead or in prison in Paraguay. Plarr remembers bitterly how his father said good-bye with a stiff upper lip to him and his mother on the quay at Asuncion twenty years ago. He lives now in a small post in Northern Argentina. He has practised as a doctor for some time at Buenos Aires and now he lives like a lonely exile in a continent of exiles. He is sad for his father and guilty because he himself is in safety and comfort. He may have sympathies for the poor, but his failure has made him devoid of emotion. He is described as a cold fish by Fortnum. The cold detachment of his medical practice has lent cynicism and lack of faith to him. He cannot believe in God or get himself involved in men's troubles. Like Fowler, he is deeply suspicious of emotional involvements. Caring is a dangerous thing according to him. Yet he cannot resist being concerned, when he learns that Fortnum, the honorary consul, is by mistake kidnapped by Paraguayan terrorists. Plarr's father is in a Paraguayan prison and, if he is alive, the kidnapping may be the last chance for his release. His humanity makes him feel responsible for the lives of Clara, Fortnum's wife and Leon Rivas, his old school friend. His father dies trying to escape, and he himself is killed.

Leon Rivas in the same novel, demonstrates the futility of human hopes. As a schoolboy, he wanted to be an "abagado" so that he could fight for the downtrodden poor and innocent. When he became a priest, he could not bear to see poverty and oppression all around him. He left the priesthood and married. Excommunicated by the Church, he became a political terrorist, heading a plot against General Stroessner. The boyhood hope to fight for the cause of the poor was strong in him, but he was too soft and gentle to be a successful "abagado." He would have been better as a priest. He could not muster revolutionary detachment to carry out the execution of Fortnum., He was carried off by sympathy. He realized that the Church is quite incapable of solving present-day problems with a practical insight. Rivas failed on both counts as abagado and a priest.

Greene's anti-heroes are failures because they are in wrong jobs which do not suit their temperament, or because they are paralysed by circumstances that disorient them. They feel they can take no sides in an issue and let things drift to rot for a while till a sense of humanity forces them to be involved and it proves their undoing. It is pity that draws them out of their uninvolvement and usually plunges them to their own ends. Fowler for example kept reiterating that he would not be committed, but Alden Pyle's 'innocent' harmfulness in killing Vietnamese for the cause of democracy forces Fowler to get Pyle killed by the communists. Fowler himself dies in the end. Doctor Plarr in *The Honorary Consul* is saddened by his father's fate and gives up interest or involvement, but acts in the end when he sees a chance of saving his father, Leon Rivas and Fortnum's wife, Clara. He dies for it.

Leon Rivas in *The Honorary Consul* failed as a priest, fails as a revolutionary too. His pity for Fortnum proves his undoing leading to death. Dr. Czinner of *Stamboul Train* too dies fighting for his people who fail to help him in his plans to lead a communist uprising. Querry in *A Burnt-Out Case*, trying to run away from the chromium world of success and glamour is drawn into his death by his pity for Mary Rycker. Death is the finale to a life of failure. Anthony Farrant of *England Made Me*, and Jones of *The Comedians*, are innocents who go about deceiving people with lies and a mask. They die for their innocence.

"D" is *The Confidential Agent* (1939) who was really a lecturer in the University of Zed and had edited an important manuscript of the "Song of Roland," left this career to devote himself to helping his political party. His failure stems from the fact that as a man who was devoted to academic pursuits he could not become ruthless enough to play a confidential agent. Failure stalks him at every step. He lands in England to contract a coal deal for his country with British mine-owners. He is hunted by enemy agents, led by an aristocrat, L. and beaten up and shot at. In fact, his own government is mistrustful of him and he is continually double-crossed by fellow agents. He feels very isolated and lonely, not at all cut out for the job of a confidential agent. He carries violence with him wherever he goes. This paralyses his will and demoralizes him completely. His wife was a victim of war. The innocent girl Else whom he befriends at the hotel is murdered. He feels responsible for the poor and miserable and this is the only reason which motivates him and makes him engage. He pities Rose Cullen, the lonely, unhappy daughter of Lord Benditch. A redeeming feature to his career is that in the end he gets the coal mines blocked by the gang of youngsters at Benditch and causes the death of Mr. K. He wins half a victory when his rival L's contract for the coal is cancelled. He does not get the coal himself. In the end, he escapes death. But this happy ending in no way qualifies him for the label of success, because, on the whole the author depicts him as made up of unwinning traits. David Pryce Jones confirms this view:

For both D and Rose are Greene's declasses, separated from their origins by inclination and intelligence, but unable to accommodate themselves afresh because the world is changing too fast to allow anybody to grow roots. . . . They belong with Coral, with Anthony and Kate, Conrad Drover and Raven: a growing band of emotionally dispossessed, fretful and fretted social orphans, unable to stabilise themselves in a vast game of snakes and ladders played by unseen strangers throwing invisible dice. . . . These declasses of both novels and entertainments are not only personally inhibited, but further restricted by the social order of this world, which is seen to destroy any natural disposition to happiness or enjoyment. They are the sad agents of disaster.[45]

There are other minor failures in other works. They may be briefly sketched. In 1936, "A Chance for Mr. Lever" appeared. Mr. Lever found himself at the end of his tether. For thirty years he had sold heavy machinery in the West and now he was dumped in an African forest feeling monotonous and melancholy. Was it fair that after thirty years he should have to go from door to door begging for a job? He had been left behind full of the taste of failure.

Mr. Chalfont in *Jubilee* (1936) instead of going to the Jubilee, stayed in bed eating ham rolls and heating the iron. He met a vulgar woman named Amy who made money by opening brothels. She pitied him and offered him money.

Chalfont was a Minty who had chosen to be gigolo rather than a newsman.[46]

The Boy of the play, *Carving a Statue,* echoes Greene's unfulfilled childhood ambitions of joining the Nigerian Navy. He says:

I wanted to be a sailor once. You've seen how good I am at knots. I had dreams of ports like Valparaiso. But all I want now is a borrowed bed and a room over the petrol pumps.[47]

Failure, betrayal and death follow each other in corollary sequence. For Greene, this had become the unremitting logic of life in his earliest intuitions. Despite all his professional success, a sense of the failure of human existence to solve all its myriads of problems, haunts him.

In the moment of the highest acclaim for his creative genius, when Greene has received recognition from different sides as one of the greatest writers in English today, the shadow of failure falls over him. To some extent it is comparable to that of Doctor Benjamin Jowett, in Greene's play, *The Great Jowett.* Jowett becomes, in spite of his enemies, Master of Balliol. He is a great scholarly success. His "Plato" is published and when Balliol Hall is built his thumb mark is fossilized in stone in the College forever. It might have seemed to everyone Jowett's day of triumph when he was receiving recognition from the Archbishop of Canterbury as the statesman, the poet, the churchman, but the sense of inadequacy, of failure in the form of early shortcomings in life, still lurked in him. He tells his valet:

> You know, Mathew, no day passes when I don't feel the defects of early education. I was never taught how to play at chess, or even at billiards, and it seems too late now. Do you think I could learn to waltz.[48]

In Jowett and in all Greene heroes, we may be up against one of Graham Greene's great paradoxical beliefs as voiced through Rose in *The Living Room:*

> Oh, we read about God's successes. We don't read about His failures. His happy failures. Who just don't care much about Him and go on living quietly all the same.[49]

And to this James replies:

One has to deserve to be a failure.[50]

The worldly success he has achieved is eclipsed by the failure to find the key that will make this life on earth meaningful. This then is the aboriginal calamity mankind is doomed for. He sensed it as a child. The scenes of death and violence lent support to it—the dead dog under a pram, with no emotion attached to the scene, the man who ran out of a house with a knife to kill himself. Greene's autobiography ends on the same note of failure that began his life. It is a reflection he makes while visiting a friend in Siam. It implicates the human race in a world-wide fiasco:

> The writer has the braggart's excuse. Knowing the unreality of his success he shouts to keep his courage up. There are faults in his work which he alone detects: even his unfavourable critics miss them. . . . We were happy that long evening, as we passed the pipe to and fro and the small flame licked upwards towards the seed of opium and the shadow moved on Buddha's fat complacent face and we talked cheerfully of the past and analysed our differing failures without guilt or regret. Hadn't Buddha failed too? The starving, the sick and the mutilated dogs lay around his temple where the yellow-robed shaven priests picked their proud way.[51]

The obsession with failure in Greene's world view in his novels, operates also at the level of human plans, institutions, government and law-enforcing systems. The failure of the Carlist Exiles' plot in *Rumour at Nightfall*, the betrayal of the smugglers' gang in *The Man Within*, the failure of Farrel's attempt to fly across the Atlantic in *The Bear Fell Free*, the failure of communism in Vietnam in *The Quiet American*, and the failure of justice in *It's a Battlefield* are just some glaring examples of the superficiality and disillusionment of human activities. The powers of Good fail miserably in the face of the world's Evil. Destiny of circumstances makes a mockery of all human endeavour.

We may aptly conclude with a passage from Henry

Newman's Poem "Pro Vita Sua" which Greene quotes in *The Lawless Roads*. It summarizes the terrible sense of failure experienced by Greene in childhood:

> To consider the world in its length and breadth . . . the greatness and littleness of man, his far-reaching aims, his short duration, the curtain hung over his futurity, the disappointment of life, the defeat of good, the success of evil, physical pain, mental anguish, the prevalence and intensity of sin. . . . All this is a vision to dizzy and appal and inflicts upon the mind the sense of a profound mystery, which is absolutely beyond human solution. . . .
>
> What shall be said to this heart-piercing reason-bewildering fact? I can only answer that either there is no Creator or this living society of man is in a true sense discarded from His presence—if, there be a God, since there is a God, the human race is implicated in some terrible aboriginal calamity.[52]

NOTES

1. Greene, Graham, *A Sort of Life,* Penguin, London, p. 16.
2. Sikiorski, Radek in *The Sunday Statesman,* May 27, 1984, p. 8.
3. Ibid., p. 8.
4. Wilson,Angus, *The Sunday Statesman,* Literary Supplement, September 30, 1984, p. 1.
5. Ayer, A.J. in *The Sunday Statesman,* Literary Supplement, September, 30,1984, p. 1.
6. Muggeridge, Malcolm in *The Sunday Statesman,* Literary Supplement, September 30, 1984, p. 1.
7. Das Gupta, Amalendu in *The Sunday Statesman*, Literary Supplement, September 30, 1984. p. 1.
8. Atkins, John, *Graham Greene*, Calder and Boyars, London,

1957, p. xiii.
9. Greene, Graham *A Sort of Life*, Penguin, p. 80.
10. Greene, Graham, interview by Radek Sikiorski in *The Sunday Statesman*, May 27, 1984, p. 8.
11. Atkins, John, p. 12.
12. Greene Graham. *A Sort of Life*, p. 9.
13. Atkins, John, *Graham Greene*, pp. 66-67.
14. Greene, Graham, *A Sort of Life*, p. 80.
15. Ibid., p. 80.
16. Greene, Graham, *Ways of Escape*, Bodley Head, London 1980, pp. 12-13.
17. Ibid., p. 20.
18. Ibid., p. 11.
19. Ibid., p. 12.
20. Ibid., p. 11.
21. Ibid.
22. Ibid., p. 52.
23. Greene, Graham, *England Made Me*, Heinemann London, 1955,
24. Ibid.
25. Ibid., p. 208.
26. Jones, Davis, *Graham Greene*, Oliver and Boyd, London, 1963.
27. Greene, Graham, *England Made Me*.
28. Ibid.
29. Greene, Graham *It's a Battlefield*, Heinemann (Uniform Ed.) London, 1956, p. 84.
30. Ibid., pp. 147-48.
31. Ibid
32. Greene, Graham, *The Power and the Glory*, Heinemann London, 1940, p. 165.
33. Ibid., p. 83.
34. Ibid., p. 80.
35. Ibid., p. 273.
36. Greene, Graham, *Stamboul Train*, Heinemann, London, 1959, p. 201.

37. Ibid., p. 79.
38. Greene, Graham. *A Burnt-Out Case,* Reprint Society, London, 1962.
39. Greene, Graham, *The Quiet American,* Heinemann, London 1960, p. 27.
40. Ibid., pp. 42-43.
41. Ibid., p. 72.
42. Ibid., pp. 49-50
43. Greene, Graham, *The Comedians,* The Bodley Head, London, 1966, p. 198.
44. Ibid., pp. 33-34.
45. Pryce Jones, David, *Graham Greene*, Oliver and Boyd, Edinburgh, 1963, p. 64.
46. Atkins, John, p. 63.
47. Greene, Graham, "Carving a Statue," in *Three Plays*, Marcury Books, London, 1961, p. 30.
48. Greene Graham, *The Great Jowett,* Radio Play, B.B.C. Pvt. Ltd. Stephen Foster, 1981, p. 40.
49. Greene Graham, "The Living Room," in *Three Plays*, p. 25.
50. Ibid.
51. Greene, Graham, *A Sort of Life*, pp. 156-57.
52. Newman, Henry, "Pro Vita Suo" quoted by Graham Greene, *The Lawless Roads,* Heinemann, London, 1954, p. 10.

The Baize Door of Childhood: The Divided Self

> *One was an inhabitant of both countries. On Saturday and Sunday afternoon of one side of the baize door, the rest of the week of the other. How can life on a border be other than restless?*[1]

Graham Greene studied at Berkhamstead School, where his father was headmaster. His family's living rooms were separated from the school dormitories by a green baize door. Either side of this door represented two different worlds, two experiences in antithesis. The family quarters stood for innocence, untainted childhood; the dormitories represented a world of evil where no one was ever quiet at the same time. Foul smells filled the air, lavatories had no locks and there were frighteningly mature schoolfellows who had "about them the general quality of evil."[1]

This early experience of two worlds of duality in nature became the defining image of all later experience for Graham Greene. The green baize door became a symbol of the intersection between hell and heaven. Indiscipline and naughtiness are common to school-life, but Greene was precociously sensitive and saw beyond the signs of the present and was able to sense the dichotomy of evil and good, an ambivalence inherent in life. This perception so influenced him at that formative, impressionable age that it moulded and defined all his secular and religious views. The green baize door is the starting point which condemned Greene to a complexity in matters of theology and this has baffled the Catholic Church and Greene's critics. His pronouncements on evil, sin, sinners, human suffering, sex, success, loyalty, justice are all informed with ambivalence. His fiction rests on the counter-pointing of antithetical orders. Thus, the religious and the secular, Catholicism and Communism, Faith and Materialism, the Secular and Divine Powers are placed on either side of the chess-borad. Each is opposed to and yet complementary to the other. One move on one side is balanced by a countermove on the other. Says Peter Kemp reviewing Greene's latest book, *The Other Man* in *The Listener:*

> .... his prose—packed with paradox and oxymoron—likes to jump backwards and forwards between contrasting ideas, with pity becoming cruel, murder kind, pleasure painful. Opposing creeds also get counterpointed—especially Catholicism and Marxism. And in these novels where sex and death, love and cynicism, commitment and infidelity are juxtaposed compulsively, the tone flickers too between hilarity and horror. It is no accident that one of Greene's grimmest books should be called 'The Comedians.' Nor does he observe the conventional barrier between the 'serious' novel and the adventure story. His books vault energetically across it.[3]

The story of *The Tenth Man* (1986) set in France under occupation, amply exemplifies this paradox. Some Germans have been killed by the Resistance and as reprisal, one out of ten French hostages in prison are going to be shot. The prisoners draw lots among themselves to decide the victims. In one of the draws, a rich Paris lawyer, Louis Chavel, becomes the tenth man. But he wants his life and sells his entire property including a country house to one of the other prisoners who is a low-paid clerk in a green-grocery. Janvier bequeathes his newly acquired property to his poor mother and sister and dies without regrets. Chavel, now free, turns up at his countryhouse as a tramp called Charlot. Janvier's mother and sister have moved into the house and Charlot is engaged as a help. The sister is full of hatred for Chavel who arranged her brother's death.

The moral hunt now begins. Ashok Mitra in a review of the book, describes it thus:

A two-way atonement is on: Chavel atoning for his sin, and the sister atoning for her hatred: one person trying to rise above his moral cowardice, the other one trying to ride out her righteous scorn. The denouement is brought about by the instrusion of a collaborationist escaping from the members of the Resistance. He pretends to be Chavel and is on the point of winning over the sister, who has by now fully purged herself of her hatred. The real Chavel feels compelled to reveal his identity. A shoot-out follows, and he dies: the cycle of atonement is complete.

But is it atonement; even if it is, is it redemption? Graham Greene does not tell us. In fact, he never does.

The format hardly matters, through the near-sixty years of his career as a writer, Graham Greene has pursued his fixed exploration. Is there a dividing line between passion and dispassion? Should one judge as one oneself would like to be judged, or should not one judge at all? Is the chasm between good and evil, between love and hate, only allegorical, and the battlefield only an illusion of the mind? 'We think there's a meaning but then we find the facts are wrong—there just isn't one. You wake with a pain and afterwards you think that was love—but the facts don't fit,' says Chavel, masquerading as Charlot, at one point in the story. That pain could be hate as well, and the facts will again perhaps refuse to fit.

Likewise, his heroes or rather anti-heroes, have dual personalities and are built up of opposing traits. For them life is one big battleground in which Good and Evil, Right and Wrong, Idealism and Cynicism are arrayed opposite each others. Peter Kemp further writes:

> Nor are Greene's characters, merely prone to geographical strayings. They also tend to slide away from partners and creeds. Attachment—political, religious and emotional is

always working loose. Betrayals and lapsed loyalties, adulteries and espionage, abound. Faith and Fidelity are alike elusive. Unreserved commitment proves almost impossible to sustain. In the divided boyhood of Graham Greene, it can be seen, fiction obsessed with Judas figures, was born. The dubious and the doubting attract his keenest interest. For him, he explains here, the novelist whose, 'station is on the ambiguous borderline between the just and the unjust, between doubt and clarity,' must be able to switch over, to change sides at the drop of a hat.'[4]

The image of the baize door, a symbol of partition between two worlds or realities recurs in Graham Greene's short story, "The Basement Room." Philip Lane, the little boy left between servants by his parents who have gone off on a holiday finds the baize door the limit he has ever touched all his nursery years. On the other side of it was the basement forbidden to him. As soon as he ventures to cross that baize door he is up against experience. His innocence confronts sin in the form of physical lust:

> His brain filled with images of all that might be wrong. He ran to the baize door and the stairs. The girl was already there and Baines was kissing her.[5]

A green baize door also exists in the sanatorium in *The Ministry of Fear*. Rowe decides to get into the sick bay at his sanatorium.

> Ahead of him was the green baize door he had never seen opened, and beyond that door lay the sick bay. He was back in his own childhood breaking out of the dormitory, daring more than he really wanted to dare, proving himself.[6]

The passage is strongly reminiscent of Greene's own school. It is obvious that the dormitories had for him a very sordid, sinful and soulless association and so he equates them with "the sick bay" where mentally retarded or disturbed people existed.

The two sides of the green baize door have both a spiritual as well as spatial meaning for Greene. In fact, in Greene's books Hell and Heaven are territories on earth where God and the Devil have separate sway. Peter Kemp, writes in *The Listener:*

> Stepping through the green baize door that separated home from school, Greene was tensely aware of crossing a boundary, traversing the dangerous edge of things. This awareness everywhere informs his books. Frontiers and boundaries stretch menacingly across his narratives; ports and customs-sheds loom prominently; escaping across a border can be a matter of life or death for his protagonists.[7]

Thus in *The Lawless Roads,* Mexico and the U.S.A. lie on either side of the border. Entering Mexico from the American side, Greene experienced the same rather vague sensations of passing from one human state of being to another as when he went to Liberia. The border represented the green baize door of his childhood. It (the door) was in a passage near his father's study. On one side were the croquet lawn, the raspberry canes, the green-house, the tennis court, his mother's bedroom; on the other, the school orchestra, matron's room, the changing rooms, the classrooms. Each side became associated with different smells, and passing from Liverpool to Freetown in *Journey Without Map* and from the U.S.A. across the bridge into Mexico, was like passing from one childhood world through the green baize door to another. Greene's crossing of this door in childhood represented ranges of human sensibility and experience, even when the crude human apparatus could not understand them clearly.

Any attempt to see the scientific equivalence between the two worlds of childhood and the geographical demarcations found later on in his books may prove frustrating. For instance, on the Mexican border there are two little frontier towns facing each other like twins and seemingly identical, but on close observation they are finely differentiated. The travellers expect to find everything changed across the border but they find the same shabbiness, a little less pronounced perhaps. The money-changers' booths in Laredo form a whole street running downhill to the international bridge and uphill on the other side into Mexico. When one reaches Novo Laredo one finds dirt and darkness. The contrast is equally vague in his story "Across the Border." A detective who is looking for an embezzler crosses into Mexico. He hopes things will be brighter and gayer this side of the frontier, but he notices that ostensibly there is no change. Perhaps what appeared worse may be better. It is difficult to compare Greene's feelings about the bridge and the green baize door. At times they appear to conflict, we are not always sure which side of the door corresponds to which side of the frontier. All we can say for sure is that it is a symbol of some experience. He uses symbols which possess a kind of protean power but which are not tied to any external meaning. It is something that does not surrender to words exactly. All told the symbol indicates a paradox or antinomy in everything Greene sees.

The ambivalence regarding sex and failure has already been elaborated upon in previous chapters. Now we can discuss his paradoxical views about (a) Sin, Sinner and Grace; (b) Human Justice, (c) Communism and Marxism, (d) His Loyalty to the Catholic Church, we can then go on to study his characters like Francis Andrews and Anthony Farrant who have dual personalities.

Greene brings out his views in his novels by counter-pointing opposing creeds and ideologies in representative characters. Thus his views about Sin, Sinners and Grace are brought out in the interplay of antithetical and sometimes complementary characters of (i) The Lieutenant and the Priest in *The Power and the Glory*, (ii) Rose and Pinkie or Rose and Ida Arnold in *Brighton Rock*. He uses his characters as embodiments of religious contradictions. Thus Sarah and Bendrix in *The End of the Affair*, the Priest in *The Power and the Glory* and Pinkie in *Brighton Rock* are persons whose souls are battlegrounds where human and divine powers wrestle with each other for supremacy. Greene's views on religious matters appear contradictory and baffling to many, especially Catholics who are used to conventional interpretations of dogma. But a close look at the genesis of Greene's religious awareness will help to explain his attitude to religion. At School, Greene had mystical experience of the true complementary nature of Good and Evil as interdependent and co-existing. This awareness was divorced from rationalization and conventional conditioning of mind. He experienced what was above religious dogma, the tenuous demarcation between Heaven and Hell, Sin and Goodness:

> It was an hour of release—and also an hour of prayer. One became aware of God with an intensity—time hung suspended—music lay on the air; anything might happen before it became necessary to join the crowd across the border. There was no inevitability anywhere . . . faith was almost great enough to move mountains . . . the great buildings rocked in the darkness. And so faith came to one—shapelessly without dogma, a presence above a croquet lawn, something associated with violence, cruelty, evil across the way. One began to believe in heaven because one believed in hell, but for a long while it was only hell one could picture with a certain intimacy—the pitchpine partitions of dormitories where everybody was never quiet at the same time, lavatories without locks.[8]

This passage reveals the peculiarity of his awareness of faith. It was a mystical realization transcending his senses, it came "shapelessly without dogma," and the important difference was that it was "associated with violence, cruelty, evil," and that he was comparatively more certain of the existence of hell than of heaven. So, here is the clue to his religious ambiguity. His theological pronouncements confound and often irritate and anger staunch Catholics, because based on Catholic dogma though they are, they invert the dogma. In prying into the heart of the matter, one is bound to see truth which mere dogma cannot define. In practice, no easy, convenient explanation of life will work. So what crops up is a seeming contradiction. Like E.M. Forster, Greene's religious stance has been "Lord,—I disbelieve—help thou my unbelief." Francis L. Kunkel supports this view:

> We should not infer that Greene is, in any sense, a propagandist for the Church. Far from offering Catholicism as a panacea, he often presents it as if it were a season in hell.[9]

Many critics who have called Greene a Catholic novelist, have ignored the fact that his conversion to Catholicism took place when he was twenty-two. It has little to do with his real religious beliefs. Greene became a Catholic because of an intellectual process of rationalization after the religion of his birth Anglican Protestantism failed to satisfy him. He discussed matters with a Catholic priest, Father Trollope for three months and was then received into the Catholic Church in February 1926. Greene's conversion was a result of frustration from one set of beliefs. Therefore, the conversion could not be permanently satisfying. It only substituted, for him, another set of beliefs. But no rationalization can give one an answer to ultimate causes. Rationalization or intellectualizing is merely surface-deep. What affects and really touches the soul is awareness of a truth. And Greene had moments of faith as a child, much earlier than the time of his conversion. David Pryce-Jones, has the same view of the early shaping of Greenc' consciousness:

> There can be no doubt that the symbols of the Christian religion have had an imaginative impact on Greene. But they have been superimposed on a personal vision which existed before conversion and which Greene has described in 'The Lost Childhood.' Some aspects of Catholic religion have corresponded to this vision, and for instance, it would be easy to say that Greene has adapted the doctrine of Original Sin for his own use. But it is more complicated than that, for Greene has subverted the doctrine for his own use.[10]

In *The Lawless Roads,* Greene tells us that the primary symbols of Hell and Heaven, of Good and Evil were altered later when he was gradually converted to Roman Catholicism:

> The Mother of God took the place of the brass eagle; one began to have a dim conception of the appalling mysteries of love moving through a ravaged world—the Cure d'Ars admitting to his mind all the impurity of a province, Peguy challenging God in the cause of the damned. It remained something one associated with misery, violence, evil.[11]

Thus in his conversion he merely found a confirmation of what he had perceived in mystical ways earlier. J.P. Kulshreshta writes:

> Vexed by the problems of evil and suffering, Greene found 'the hint of an explanation' in the Roman Catholic Church. It may, however, be stated that Greene's sense of evil cannot be attributed to his adopted religion. His sense of evil, already obsessive, was caught up in his conversion and . . . in so far as it is now religious it does not strike one as specifically Roman Catholic.[12]

With this childhood background, we are in a better position to understand his religious ambivalence. For sinners in his world, Greene plays a Devil's advocate, much like Milton does for Satan in *Paradise Lost*. Thus Greene's sinners are much loved by God. Grace usually comes to such people. Francis L. Kunkel says:

> A Catholic novelist in the profound sense will, as Greene does, linger at the intersection where God confronts man and grace encounters free will. Sufficient cooperation with divine grace will work miracles. It will change an adulteress into a holy woman (Sarah), and a brandy-bibber into a martyr (the anonymous priest).[13]

Ironically Greene's Catholic characters are his greatest sinners. And sinners are God's favourites. God stalks them like the Hound of Heaven to gain their soul by his grace. Like a divine rival for their love, He wrests them from their human lovers. Thus, in *The End of the Affair*, God reaches out to Sarah in her hell of lust and adultery and she succumbs to him. She loved Bendrix passionately, but when he is knocked out by a bomb-blast, she is ready to give up her physical lust for Bendrix if God would bring Bendrix back to life.

> Let him be alive, and I will believe. . . . I said very slowly, I'll give him up for ever, only let him be alive with a chance.[14]

Her prayer is answered. Bendrix recovers, and she gives herself upto God and believes. God gains His victory. In fact, to many critics, God's reaching out in grace to an adulteress is an idea so baffling to conventionally-minded Christians that critics have mockingly stated that the theme of *The End of the Affair* is "Adultery Leads to Sainthood." Donat O'Donnell has described the love-lust interchangeability in Greene's works in the form of a pseudo-syllogism:

> Passion is the name of the sufferings of Christ on the cross. Passion is the name of a certain kind of sexual desire, ergo a certain kind of sexual desire is the same as the sufferings of Christ on the cross.[15]

But this is a misunderstanding, a simplification of the issue. A sinner does not gain God's love merely by an easy act of submission to His Will. The God-acceptance brings in its wake terrible suffering. The soul is tortured between the pulls of the flesh and the promptings of the divine.

> In the shadow of plenitude, no quarter is given to the ecstasy of the flesh which must be replaced by the agony of the spirit. Faith brings in its wake an awful deprivation, the dark night of the soul, to Sarah. She undertakes the journey which St. John of the Cross describes in 'The Ascent of Mt. Carmel.'[16]

In fact, here is the inherent paradox. Suffering is an indispensable part of the process of ascent to God or to the divine plane of life.

Francis L. Kunkel makes the ambivalence clear in a few clear flourishes:

> Sarah Miles in 'The End of the Affair,' is a carefree sinner before her conversion and life of virtue plunge her into woe. The nearer she approaches to God, the less joy she takes from the created world and human love. And the more the anonymous priest, in 'The Power and the Glory,' comports himself in keeping with Catholic precepts, the greater the suffering he is called upon to endure. Pascal, in his 'Pensees,' describes the wretchedness of man without God; Greene describes the wretchedness of man with God.[17]

God's love of sinners, (like Christ's love of the pharisees), includes Pinkie, the juvenile criminal of *Brighton Rock,* the nameless priest in *The Power and the Glory,* and Scobie, the unfaithful Deputy Commissioner of Police in *The Heart of the Matter.*

The Priest is a whisky-addict, has sired an illegitimate daughter, Brigitta, and is painfully aware of having failed God. But God seeks just these vessels, broken and unworthy, to find a house in. The Priest's humility about his failings and his spiritual suffering gradually transform him. Before his execution, in the police station, looking at his own portrait of the halcyon Concepcion days, the priest realizes the paradoxical nature of the change which sin and suffering have wrought in his life. From comparative innocence and smug indifference to other people's pain, he has moved on to corruption and involvement in human misery.

> That was another mystery. It sometimes seemed to him that venial sins—impatience, an unimportant lie, pride, a neglected opportunity—cut you off from grace more completely than the worst sins of all. Then, in his innocence, he had felt no love for anyone, now in his corruption he had learnt.[18]

Greene's baize door was not merely a dividing line between two sets of beliefs (represented by two antithetical characters) but it was also a converging point where two opposing orders faced each other and found reflection of one in the other. Thus opposites complement each other in Greene's view. When the Whisky Priest goes with the Mestizo to give absolution to a dying gangster the priest feels the pull of a fellow-being in life's journey. When the gangster dies unrepentant, asking him to 'beat it,' the priest thinks:

> At best, it was only one criminal trying to aid the escape of another—whichever way you looked, there wasn't much merit in either of them.[19]

The priest's suffering for his own sins shows humility and repentance. Besides, he dies in order to save a damned gangster. He risked his life to the police by going to the dying man. This shows his faith in his religious vocation despite his personal despondency. These facts, therefore, elevate him to sainthood in Greene's eyes. Herbert Haber says that the priest found the way to martyrdom "through an immersion in the pentecostal flame of earthly sin."[20]

Greene's seeming paradox lies in the belief that in reaching the depths of despair and frustration, one finally surrenders oneself to God's will. There are echoes, here, of St. Augustine:

> "Thou hast made us for Thee, O Lord! And our hearts are restless until they rest in Thee."

Frederick R. Karl, has explained the Greenesque inversion in a lucid light:

> Because Greene believes that from impurity will come purity, from demonism saintliness, from unbelief belief, from vice virtue, his 'heroes' often seem closer to demons than to saints. Nearly every serious Greene protagonist, despite external expedience and even personal degradation has a vision of saintliness, while his inner conflict, often not apparent to him, results from his inability to live up to his ideal. In these terms Greene places the tension between pride and moderation,

> analogous to the conflict of the Greek tragic hero. Like Oedipus, whose pride has overwhelmed his sense of reasonableness, Scobie, Pinkie and the whiskey priest, for example, all recognize how far short they have fallen of the ideal, how mortal they are.[20]

Pinkie, the delinquent criminal and Scobie who commits adultery, show the strange, inscrutable workings of divine love and mercy. Despite their heinous sins, no one can pass a judgement consigning them to Hell. According to Greene, God's mercy transcends conventional, human criteria. It reaches out to the worst sinner, who having gone the whole hog through sin and having run the full circle of the compass of sin, confronts God. That is the nature of the "appalling strangeness" of God's mercy. Louise believes that her husband, Scobie (in *The Heart of the Matter)* is damned. But Father Rank thinks otherwise. He is Greene's mouthpiece:

> For goodness sake, Mrs. Scobie, don't imagine you—or I—know a thing about God's mercy. . . . The Church knows all the rules. But it doesn't know what goes on in a single human heart.[22]

Thus Greene's childhood vision, the baize door factor, brings two opposing facts to face each other, often to blend across the passage that demarcates one world from another. Thus, a sinner in his love, lustful though it be, finds himself face to face with God who offers His Hand in succour.

Like Sarah, Scobie and the Priest, Pinkie, too, comes in for God's consideration of mercy, despite his satanic sinfulness. But, he is the only one, who defies the Hound of Heaven and escapes into damnation.

> Like Dostoevsky's Stavrogin, he has denied himself not only the good but also repentance, the possibility of forgiveness.[23]

Driving out of Brighton with Rose, he feels grace reaching for him like "the pressure of gigantic wings against the glass,"[24] but he withstands it

> With all the bitter force of the school bench, the cement playground, the St. Pancras waiting room. . . .[25]

This childhood essence of abandonment fought against grace and won. He is "whipped away into Zero-nothing."

Rose is certain that Pinkie is damned, but the priest (Greene's spokesman) thinks otherwise. He gives her hope through the story of a Frenchman called Charles Peguy:

> He was a good man, a holy man, and he lived in sin through all his life because he couldn't bear the idea that any soul should suffer damnation. . . . He never took the sacraments. He never married his wife in Church. I don't know, my child, but some people think he was . . . well, a saint.[26]

One inference, ambivalent in nature, has been drawn by critics from Greene's concept of divine mercy. This is that corruption is "a sort of backhanded tribute to God; it is even a form of godliness to be corrupt, or at least to be corrupt does not deprive us of a form of godliness."[27] In fact, God uses unworthy sinners like Rose in *Brighton Rock* and the Whiskey Priest to carry on His work of redemption. This implication drawn by certain critics is an oversimplification of the issue, and shows lack of deep research. God does not love evil for its own sake just to prove, as it were, a haphazard working of His powers. Beyond the intellectual grasp of man's limited mind though God may be, it is not correct to say that Greene advocates an eccentric, topsy-turvy doctrine merely to catch our attention. Thus, corruption is not a tribute to God. The heart of the matter is that men are drawn away to evil and corruption by the circumstances of life and this going astray from the path of righteousness, shows a soul's disappointment; it implies his love of an ideal he could not achieve. "The very terms of denial contain the seeds of attachment."[28] In the quagmire of corruption, where the injured soul wallows, he suffers and suffering brings to the surface an awareness of deeper issues lying between man and God. Thus, there is a confrontation with God's mercy. At the point of intersection, where Hell and Heaven meet, in the passage at Greene's childhood home where Good and Evil met at the baize door, the corrupted man, having travelled the full length of sin, finally reaches God. Sarah, Scobie, Pinkie, the Whiskey Priest show the failure of an ideal, which works to corrupt and destroy their pride in strange ways and finally make them helplessly aware of their limitations and resign them to God's will. It is only then that they become fit receptacles for God's grace. Frederick Karl explains the process of sanctification of a sinner in an analogy to the Greek idea.

> Greene's belief that failure is nearer God than the success is of course close to the Greek idea of hubris; in this view, the successful, boasting man, full of overweening pride, challenges the order of the universe by considering himself greater than the gods, and at this point, when he attempts to expand from man-size to god-size, at the very apex of pride and vanity, he is struck down. Thus also within the Christian world, God operates, although he retains sympathy and pity for the failure, for the one struck down. In such a view Greene is closer to Dostoevsky and Mauriac.[29]

The fall of man is exemplified in the Whiskey Priest. Proud and complacent, receiving honours as a priest in Concepcion, he was far removed from his Christian ideal. But he falls miserably, siring an illegitimate daughter Brigitta and is given to excessive drinking. He becomes constantly aware of his fall and the paradox is that while the devil completely possesses him he becomes ready for sainthood. This is what Greene means when he speaks through the mouth of James, a character in *The Living Room:*

> There's one thing I remember from the seminary. I've forgotten nearly all the things they taught me, even the arguments

for the existence of God. It comes from the book of devotion: 'The more our senses are revolted, uncertain and in despair, the more surely faith says: 'This is God: all goes well.'[30]

Like the Whiskey Priest, Querry in *A Burnt-Out* Case receives a similar accolade from Father Thomas. Querry is desperately tired of the world, a man at the end of his tether who realizes what an arid life he has reached by the meaningless success of his worldly ambitions. In Africa, he feels drawn out of himself by a reawakening of his interest in the lepers who suffer. Father Thomas says to Querry:

> Perhaps even now you are walking in the footsteps of St. John of the Cross, the noche oscura.[31]

Querry insists that the priest has not understood him really, but the priest is adamant. The Superior warns against recognising Querry as a living saint:

> But don't let's recognise them before the Church does.[32]

Greene's attitude to suffering is informed with ambivalence.

> Pain is part of joy. We are hungry and then think how we enjoy our food.[33]

But this is not strange to the general Christian ethic. Put more philosophically, it reminds us of the words of a great philosopher. "There are many places in a man's soul, and suffering must enter them to make them exist." The doors to many worlds of truth remain closed to the happy, smug man. Now Greene's stance is quite clear till now. But it begins to baffle some when he makes the priest in *The Power and the Glory* bid the peasants pray that they may suffer more.

> That is why I tell you that heaven is here: this is a part of

heaven just as pain is a part of pleasure.

And he continued:

> Pray that you will suffer more and more and more. Never get tired of suffering. The police watching you, the soldiers gathering taxes, the beating you always get from the Jefe because you are too poor to pay, small pox and fever, hunger . . . that is all part of heaven—the preparation.[34]

The passage is strongly reminiscent of Christ's Sermon on the Mount in which he calls those people blessed who suffer for His sake. But the difference is in Greene's twist. He invites suffering voluntarily: "Pray that you will suffer more and more." Early in childhood, Greene had discovered the pleasure of masochism, of inflicting pain on oneself. At the age of 14, he wanted to do things to a girl who lived close by:

> I didn't do anything about it. I wasn't old enough, but I was happy; I could think about pain as something desirable and not as something dreaded. It was as if I had discovered that the way to enjoy life was to appreciate pain.[35]

Suffering is a blessing in disguise that comes to the few chosen for salvation. Scobie, Bendrix, Sarah and Querry achieve the beatific consummation through a purification in the pentecostal fire of sin and suffering. They are not aware of their own redemption at the end. David Pryce-Jones uses a beautiful metaphor to picturize Greene's suffering-redemption inversion:

> Querry, then, has completed the eschatological somersault, and comes the right way up at his death. He has rounded off the movement started by the priest who leapt for sanctification, continued by Scobie who failed in the pain of the exercise, hated by Bendrix who comprehended the full evolution, and shirked by Fowler at the peril of personal empti-

> ness. In this fearful gymnasium erected by God, suffering is what we are expected to perform—such is the moral of these almost masochistic religious gymnasts and it will involve this ambiguous attitude to the coach.[36]

To many people who would take the direct line, or conventional view in matters of religion, it again sounds a strange paradox that we should masochistically invite suffering to gain beatitude. But Greene's baize door factor from childhood places suffering and God-realization at the point of meeting for two realities. Suffering denotes the workings of conscience and spiritual guilt which help to unearth a man's despair and failures. It is, therefore, an acknowledgement of one's sins. It is the humility of this attitude that makes the soul empty of its egoistic dross finally, and makes it, in turn, an empty receptacle for God's grace to enter. Inversely, the smug, complacent, happy man is all concerned with superficial realities. He remains too proud to know his own weaknesses and is, therefore, unfit to receive the divine visitation in his heart. This paradoxical stance makes itself manifest through various statements in *The Heart of the Matter:*

> Point me out the happy man and I will point you out either egotism, evil—or else an absolute ignorance.
>
> The truth . . . has never been of any real value to any human being—it is a symbol for mathematicians and philosophers to pursue.[37]

This statement shows that Greene takes the opposite stance to that of mathematicians and philosophers. For the latter, truth is a symbol to be philosophized, but to the real truth-seeker, it is something outside statistics and formulae. It is something experienced by a soul. Thus, suffering is necessary, it is good—this is Greene's awareness.

At the time Greene wrote *A Burnt-Out Case,* his mind was working under the influence of a remarkable book written by the French biologist-priest, Teilhard de Chardin. This book, *The Phe-*

nomenon of Man had a direct influence on Greene's *A Burnt-Out Case*. Greene himself has acknowledged this fact. Chardin's book researches scientifically the necessity of evil and suffering in a universe progressing to perfection. This evolution he calls Christogenesis. Dr. Colin in *A Burnt-Out Case* echoes Chardin's view when he tries to prove the identity of religious and secular views in life. The great dichotomy that separated the worlds of childhood, "the baize door," breaks down allowing evil and suffering to appear as a continuing pattern in the carpet of good. The good and the evil, thus appear as warp and woof interwoven into the fabric of existence. Chardin's book naturally impressed Greene a lot, because in it he found an extension of his own childhood myth. The great Christian philosopher echoes strongly what Greene had intuitively known at Berkhamstead School.

> how many failures have there been for one success, how many days of misery for one hour's joy, how many sins for a solitary saint? To begin with we find physical lack-of-arrangement or derangement on the material level; then suffering which cuts into the sentient flesh; then, on a still higher level, wickedness and the torture of spirit as it analyses itself and makes choices. Statistically, at every degree of evolution, we find evil always and everywhere, forming and reforming implacably in us and around us. Necessarium est at scandala eveniant. This is relentlessly imposed by the play of large numbers at the heart of a multitude undergoing organization.... A universe which labours, which sins and which suffers. . . . Suffering and failure, tears and blood; so many by-products (often precious, moreover re-utilisable) begotten by the noosphere on its way. This, in final analysis is what the spectacle of the world in movement reveals to our observation and reflection at the first stage.[38]

Greene places antithetical religious and secular powers, often represented by individuals on either side of the "baize door" the symbolic dividing line. Then, he demolishes the "baize door," or divide and blends the opposites as complements. Thus we have the following equations:

1. Andrews versus Elizabeth (in *The Man Within)* representing lust and sanctity respectively.
2. Rose versus Pinkie, representing innocence versus experience (in *Brighton Rock).*
3. Rose/Pinkie versus Ida Annold representing the symbiosis Evil/Good versus Right/Wrong.
4. Anthony versus Kate, representing innocence and experience (in *England Made Me).*
5. The Commissioner of Police versus Caroline Bury, representing Idealism and Faith (in *It's a Battlefield).*
6. The Priest versus the Lieutenant representing Faith/Sin pitted against Empty Goodness (in *The Power and the Glory).*
7. Catholicism is pitted against Communism in Mexico in *The Lawless Roads.*
8. Communism is placed opposite American idealism in *The Quiet American.*
9. Pulling versus Aunt Augusta standing for inactive good and childhood mischievousness respectively in *Travels with My Aunt.*
10. Rivas is counterpointed against God and their relationship represents Evil versus Evolution in *The Honorary Consul.*

In all these equations, the contrast is first spelled out and then the difference is shelved, allowing each to recognize the worth of its opposite number and to see its own reflection in the other.

In *The Man Within,* Francis Andrews is painfully aware of his sinfulness. His lust for Lucy fills him with great guilt. Elizabeth is all purity and innocence and Andrews finds in her a hope for his redemption. She has all the qualities he has desired in life, but never achieved. He is drawn to her. In her he discovers "the promise of his two selves at one, the peace which he had discovered sometimes in music."[39] Thus Andrews sees his own inadequacy completed in her. In Greene, opposites are not inimical to each other in the final resort.

The friendship of Rose and Pinkie in *Brighton Rock* is "the tragic companionship of irreconcilables." Pinkie discovers in her his true complement.

> What was most evil in him needed her: it couldn't get along without goodness . . . she was good, he'd discovered that, and he was damned; they were made for each other.[40]

In the same novel, another polarity is described between two levels of reality. Pinkie and Rose represent larger issues like good and evil, while Ida Arnold advocates a philosophy that considers issues which are more mundane—right and wrong. Ida Arnold's Rabelaism, her uninhibited enjoyment of sex is set off against Pinkie's morbid cruelty and abhorrence of sex. Ida's "experience" talks to Rose, the innocent:

> 'I know one thing you don't. I know the difference between Right and Wrong. They didn't teach you that at school.'
>
> Rose didn't answer; the woman was quite right; the two words meant nothing to her. Their taste was extinguished by stronger foods—Good and Evil. The woman could tell her nothing she didn't know about these—she knew by tests as clear as mathematics that Pinkie was evil—what did it matter in that case whether he was right or wrong.[41]

Thus Pinkie and Rose represent the gloomy Brighton with its God or Devil, and Ida represents gay Brighton with its secular ethics.

In *England Made Me,* Kate acts as a foil to her brother Farrant. Whatever is weak in him, is upholstered by her love for him. Twins though they are, temperament prevents them from completely understanding each other. Anthony is an innocent abroad in Krogh's materialistic world. Kate with her sagacity and tenacity of will has developed good business sense. In fact, Kate has all the masculine virtues of reliability and efficiency whereas he has what most women desire most—charm. While Kate has developed a successful cynicism, Anthony's life has been a long line of failures. While Anthony is soft and sentimental, she can be brazen and cold-blooded. And yet each wants the other and mirrors each other's desires:

> His was the weakness which should have been hers, the uncertainty, the vanity, the charm of something rash and unpremeditated. It was the nearest she could get to completeness, having him in the same room.[42]

Faith and idealism are pitted against each other in many Greene novels. In *It's a Battlefield,* Caroline Bury and the Assistant Commissioner are on common ground when they feel a sense of waste and suffering regarding human life. But the difference between them is highlighted when Caroline Bury is buoyed up by a peculiar "faith" symbolised by incense, Indian idols, icons and pictures of the Virgin. It is faith which the Assistant Commissioner deplores he lacks. He reflects:

> It's lucky she has got faith. Whatever she means by it, she's got nothing else.[43]

The Assistant Commissioner cannot muster up faith in any directing purpose in life and there is something mercenary and unrewarding about his life:

> He fought because he was paid to fight, and only occasionally did the sight of some brutality lend conviction to the brain with which he fought.[44]

In *It's a Battlefield,* both faith and its opposite cynicism are described as inane emotions. But in Greene's religious novels—*Lawless Roads* and *The Power and the Glory*, faith is a redeeming virtue and despite its implications of sin, it wins the battle against "Empty Goodness," against secular idealism. The priest representing the religious Power of God is a man of pygmy faith and the

Lieutenant representing the limited earthly power, is a man of towering faith. While both work for good on earth, their methods differ. The priest has God's love to offer the world, the Lieutenant has his grand plans of an earthly utopia in which the Church and its religion are absent. The Priest sins and drinks, the Lieutenant is almost an ascetic, neither drinking nor having need of women. In fact, at certain stages of their interaction, they are made to recognize each other's goodness. The one reflects the other. They are in the words of A.A. Devitis:

> doubles in the Dostoevskian and Conradian sense . . . each suggesting what the other should be, each accenting the pity that is in the other while denying the evil.[45]

By clever word-play, Greene strikes parallels in the nature of the Priest and the Lieutenant. Both are tied up to a cause they cannot shirk any more. When the priest returns to the interior of the State he feels like the king of a West African tribe, the slave of his people. And the Lieutenant, walking through the town thinking of the new children in a new Tabasco, appears like "a theologian going back over the errors of the past to destroy them again." And the greatest irony is that, as Greene presents it, despite his corruption and sinfulness, the priest lives in the shadow of divinity and the Lieutenant and earthly powers cannot win it over.

In *Lawless Roads,* again, Catholicism is pitted against the banal idealism of communism. Faith, despite its sinful followers, was still preferable to materialistic idealism. Greene writes in the book:

> I loathed Mexico—but there were times when it seemed as if there were worse places. . . . Here were idolatry and oppression, starvation and casual violence, but you lived under the shadow of religion—of God or the Devil. 'Rating for Dating'—it wasn't evil, it wasn't anything at all, it was just the drugstore and the Coca-Cola, the hamburger, the sinless empty graceless chromium world.[46]

The Mexican predicament, the war between the God of faith and the Devil of the twentieth century, leads Greene to consider the modern world today in the same light of duality. It is a territory fought over by two powers:

> The world is all of a piece, of course; it is engaged everywhere in the same subterranean struggle, lying like a tiny neutral state, with whom no one ever observes his treaties, between the two eternities of pain—and God knows the opposite of pain; not we. It is a Belgium fought over by friend and enemy alike.[47]

In *Journey Without Maps,* the instinctive supernatural forces of darkness in Liberia form an antithesis to Greene's awareness of the banality of violent, sophisticated modern civilisation. The book shows that the "baize door" or barrier lies between the childhood of Man as represented in the unaffected, natural life of the African natives and the spoilt adulthood of Man as represented by civilized societies in the West. One must pass through the baize door like Greene, from modern materialism to the Dark Continent where the childhood of mankind lies still unspoiled. This dual world was to resurface in Greene's book, *A Burnt-Out Case,* in which Querry has to pass over from one world of unhappy materialistic success to another world called Pendele in Africa which puts him in touch with the childhood of the human race in the form of uninhibited dancing and singing. It is difficult to define clearly Greene's political ideology, very much in the same way as his religious creed eludes our full understanding, unless we consider it in terms of the "baize-door" symbolism. In an interview by Maria Couto, Greene says:

> Since I am critical, I am suspect from the Catholic and from the Socialist point of view; I cannot be wholeheartedly a Socialist according to a fixed Marxist standpoint or a Catholic to those who wish to extend the dogma of papal infallibility.[48]

Greene can see similarities in the views of differing creeds. His answer to the question "Don't you think Liberation Theology suggests the overlap between Marxism and Catholicism?" is

> Yes. We've got the same structures in the sense that you can compare the Curia, and the Politburo; both are bad. And I think the church today is concerned with poverty. Perhaps as the church becomes more concerned with poverty and human rights the Marxists become less concerned with poverty and there's nothing to show they are concerned with human rights. I find that the most interesting comments on my books have come from Catholics and Communists and that there is a parallel between the rather hesitant doubts of some of my Communist friends and my own doubts.[49]

But while Greene shows leanings to Marxism, and to socialism in his cry for the underdog and the common man, one cannot straighttaway proclaim him to be a communist. Recently in an interview taken by Radek Sikiorski, Greene was asked what feature of the civilization of America or Russia he disliked most. To this he replied:

> In America what I dislike most is its materialism and I don't accuse the Russians there. I have more faith in the buried religious feeling in the Russian nature than I have in an average American. Communism and capitalism reflect each other in a mirror. They often seem the same. You have Reagan talking about the 'Evil' of communism and then you have a Communist talking about the evil of capitalism. And politically you have Afghanistan on one side and El Salvador on the other.[50]

The old-world traditional Europe represented by the English journalist Fowler is opposed to Pyle's new world innocence in Greene's *The Quiet American*. Pyle is engagé or committed to the cause of American idealism and democracy, and is convinced of the necessity of saving Vietnam from the monster of communism. On the other hand, Fowler is degagé and distrusts Pyle's platitudes and all his cant of "isms" and "cracies." Fowler tells Pyle with reference to the Vietnamese:

> They want rice. They don't want to be shot at. They want one day to be much the same as another. They don't want our white skins around telling them what they want.[51]

The two views towards the succour of Vietnam are brought out by a study of contrast, of personal incompatibilities in which racial (decadent European and idealistic American) differences are implied.

Many Greene critics have opined that *The Quiet American* is inspired by Greene's anti-Americanism. Harvey Curtis Webster says:

> the Englishmen who belonged to the 'Ministry of Fear' and the Mexicans who pursued the whiskey-priest are found guilty . . . of similarly well-intentioned idealism.[52]

The two worlds of God and the Devil, good and bad are also debated by Rivas and Plarr in Greene's fictional-historical novel, *Honorary Consul.* Plarr cannot reconcile the idea of God's love and our duty to respond to that love in the light of the human experience he sees around him:

> It's like the duty of a German to love Hitler. Isn't it better not to believe in that horror up there sitting in the clouds of heaven than to pretend to love him?[53]

But Rivas can find a reconciliation between Evil and God by seeing in his own human way the dual essence of the Creator of the worlds. In fact, God is ambivalent, formed in the image of Greene, or the other way round, because God is of dual essence, so is Greene's mind. Graham Greene had read Pierre de Chardin's book, *The*

Phenomenon of Man in which Evil is described as an essential part of the process of evolution. Greene was greatly impressed by this fact. It reinforced his own dictum expressed in *The End of the Affair* and *The Power and the Glory* that suffering is indispensable for the uplift of a soul. The shadow of Chardin's book fell heavily on *A Burnt-Out Case* and on *The Honorary Consul.* Greene uses Rivas as his mouthpiece to describe a divided God:

> He made us in his image—and so our evil is His evil too. How could I love God if he were not like me? Divided like me. Tempted like me. . . . Every evil act of ours strengthens His night-side, and every good one helps His day-side. We belong to Him and He belongs to us. But now at least we can be sure where evolution will end one day—it will end in a goodness like Christ's.[54]

The paradox of Rivas is that he has to do evil out of love for those who suffer.

> A saint would only have to pray, but I have to carry a revolver. I slow evolution down.[55]

Rivas believes that evil action is necessary to strengthen God's night-side which is one aspect of evolution to perfection.

Graham Greene has admitted that since childhood he has been basically a manic-depressive, with, I should like to add, the depressive phase predominating most of the while. He says in his autobiography: "A manic-depressive, like my grand-father—that would be the verdict of me today. . . .[56] And he also states that he writes to nourish his manic-depressive temperament. Thomas Harris explains the symptoms of a manic-depressive character:

> A manic-depressive person periodically undergoes severe and unexplainable shifts in mood. In the manic, or high phase he feels euphoric, on top of the world, and full of energy. . . . Then for no reason of which he is aware he sinks into a period

of extreme depression.[57]

Greene's works reveal both aspects of his consciousness. Most of Greene's work that I have discussed so far belongs to the depressive aspect of his nature. They portray "the madness inherent in the human situation." When he wrote *May We Borrow Your Husband* and *Other Comedies of the Sexual Life*, he initiated the manic binge in his life. *Travels with My Aunt* came out in 1971 and in it the baize door separating the two worlds of innocence and experience is removed, allowing the two to become part of one territory. Henry Pulling represents a sedate, suburban world in which there is no keen pleasure, only one long drab existence. Inactive goodness pervades it. A retired bank manager in his fifties, he is a rather phlegmatic and unimaginative man. His uneventful, monotonous life in which the only excitement is a funeral is characterized by the cultivation of dahlias, the Major next door, a meal from Chicken. He has been reduced to a static life by thirty years of bank service and he dislikes the unexpected. A bachelor and misogynist, he leads a cocooned existence. His world represents the effete, dull, mechanical world of the adult whose perceptions have been flouted by too much moralizing. His world comes into touch with that of Aunt Augusta whose vibrant mode of life, all agog to the world, represents the childhood world in which enthusiasm and perceptions are still sharp and fresh. In fact, Greene's fancy here relaxes from the tension of his serious novels and even evil is equated with child-like mischief. The "baize-door" breaks down and Aunt Augusta enters Pulling's world, initiating him into her picaresque, uninhibited life. Following her like a Sancho Panza, Pulling visits all the shady haunts of Europe. He becomes extravagant and frolicsome and plunges into an underworld and becomes a smuggler in Paraguay. He has thrown morality overboard and reasons:

> I had been born as a result of what my step-mother would have called an immoral act, an act of darkness. I had begun in immoral freedom. Why then should I have found myself in a

prison-house?[58]

Inactive good merges into evil. Elizabeth Sewell's comment on Greene's work is relevant here in describing the blending of incompatible natures.

> . . . inversion, the ambivalence of attraction and repulsion, an inside-outness which gives it a strange likeness to the Looking-Glass world. . . . Evil and innocence become convertible.[59]

Greene's characters are composed of a dichotomy of human nature. In fact, Greene has shown in his works the symptoms of a split consciousness. Did he create Francis Andrews, the hero of his first successful publication, *The Man Within* in his own image? Francis Andrews is conscious always of an interior division in his person. He muses:

> It is as though there were six different people inside me. They all urge different things. I don't know which is myself.[60]

Andrews' existence is a "series of zigzags" with contradictory tendencies and "incompatible impulses."[61]

In fact, his life is lived on a precarious borderline where spirit and flesh wrestle with each other. Like Greene, Andrews exemplifies the story of "homoduplex" or the split personality. In fact, there are a number of such Greene characters including Anthony in *England Made Me* and Bendrix in *The End of the Affair*. Everywhere in Greene's world, opposites blend and attract each other. In *The Comedians,* Brown wonders how easily a rogue like Jones makes friends with good people like Mr. Smith.

> Perhaps the crooked appeals to the straight or the guilty to the innocent, like blonde appeals to black.[62]

In his autobiography, *A Sort of Life*, Greene says:

If I were to choose an epigraph for all the novels I have written, it
would be, from 'Bishop Blougram's Apology':

Our interest's on the dangerous edge of things.
The honest thief, the tender murderer,
The superstitious atheist, demi-rep
That loves and saves her soul in new French books
We watch while these in equilibrium keep
The giddy line midway.[63]

I think the lines are a fitting summary of this chapter.

NOTES

1. Greene, Graham, *The Lawless Roads*, Heinemann, London, 1954, p. 4.
2. Ibid., p. 5.
3. Kemp, Peter, "The Judas Expert," *The Listener,* 12 May, 1983, pp. 24-25.
4. Ibid., p. 24.
5. Greene, Graham, "The Basement Room" in *Modern English Short Stories,* Selected with an Introduction by Devek Hudson, Oxford University Press, Calcutta, 1970, p. 144.
6. Greene, Graham, *Ministry of Fear,* Heinemann, London (Library Ed.), 1960, p. 183.
7. Kemp, Peter, "The Judas Expert," p. 24
8. Greene, Graham, *The Lawless Roads,* pp. 4-5.
9. Kunkel, Francis L., "Graham Greene: The Anatomy of a Catholic Novelist," *Catholic Book Reporter,* May 1961, p. 8.
10. Pryce-Jones, David , *Graham Greene,* Oliver and Boyd; Edinburgh, p.
11. Greene, Graham, *The Lawless Roads*, pp. 4-5.
12. Kulshreshtha, J.P., *Graham Greene: The Novelist*, Macmil-

lan, Delhi, 1977, p. 13.

13. Kunkel, Francis L., Graham Greene: "The Anatomy of a Catholic Novelist," p. 8.
14. Greene, Graham, *The End of the Affair,* Heinemann, London (Library Ed.), 1959, p. 113.
15. O'Donnell, Donat, *Maria Cross,* London, 1953, p. 246.
16. Kulshrestha, J.P. p. 121.
17. Kunkel, Francis L., p. 8.
18. Greene, Graham, *The Power and the Glory,* Heinemann, London (Uniform Ed.), 1951, p. 166.
19. Ibid., p. 245.
20. Haber, Herbert, "The Two Worlds of Graham Greene," *Modern Fiction Studies,* Autumn, 1957, p. 266.
21. Karl, Frederick, "Greene's Demoniacal Heroes," in *The Contemporary English Novel*, Thomas & Hudson, 1972, p. 88.
22. Greene, Graham, *The Heart of the Matter.* The Reprint Society, London, 1950, p. 296.
23. Kulshrestha, J.P., p. 64.
24. Greene, Graham, *Brighton Rock,* Heinemann, London, 1955, p. 322.
25. Ibid., p. 322.
26. Ibid., p. 331.
27. Greene, Graham, "Frederick Rolfe: Edwardian Inferno" in *The Lost Childhood and Other Essays.* Eyre and Spottiswoode, London, 1951, p. 94.
28. Karl, Frederick, 88.
29. Ibid., p. 93.
30. Greene, Graham, "The Living Room," in *Three Plays,* Mercury Books, London, 1961, p. 57.
31. Greene, Graham, *A Burnt-Out Case,* The Reprint Society, London, 1962, p. 107.
32. Ibid., p. 102.
33. Greene, Graham, *The Power and the Glory,* p. 86.
34. Ibid.
35. Greene, Graham, *Journey Without Maps*, Heinemann, Lon-

don (Uniform ed.), 1950, p. 31.
36. Pryce-Jones, David, p. 97.
37. Greene, Graham, *The Heart of the Matter*, p. 70.
38. Chardin, Pierre Teilhard de, *The Phenomenon of Man*, Fontana Religious Books, 1970, pp. 340-41.
39. Greene, Graham, *The Man Within*, Heinemann, London (Uniform ed.), 1950, p. 42.
40. Greene, Graham, *Brighton Rock*, pp. 167-8.
41. Ibid., pp. 267-8.
42. Greene, Graham, *England Made Me*, Heinemann, London, 1955, p. 177.
43. Greene, Graham, *It's a Battlefield*, Heinemann, London (Uniform ed.), 1956, p. 221.
44. Ibid., p. 148.
45. Devitis, A.A., *Graham Greene*, Twayne, New York, 1964, p. 174.
46. Greene, Graham, *The Lawless Roads*, p. 234.
47. Ibid., p. 29.
48. Couto, Maria, "Excursions into Greeneland," *Express Magazine*, April 3, 1988.
49. Ibid.
50. Sikiorski, Radek, "The Heart of the Matter," *The Sunday Statesman*, Delhi, May 27, 1984, p. 151.
51. Greene, Graham, *The Quiet American*, Heinemann, London, 1960, p. 119.
52. Webster, Harvey Curtis, "The World of Graham Greene," in *Graham Greene* (ed.), R.O. Evans, p. 23.
53. Greene, Graham, *The Honorary Consul*, Penguin, London, 1964, p. 226.
54. Ibid., pp. 227-28.
55. Ibid., p. 228.
56. Greene, Graham, *A Sort of Life*, Penguin, London, 1971, p. 92.
57. Harris, Thomas, *I'm OK—You're O.K.*, Pan, London, 1977, pp. 104-5.
58. Greene, Graham, *Travels with My Aunt*, Penguin, London,

1971, p. 203.

59. Sewell, Elizabeth, "Graham Greene" in *Dublin Review,* CCXXVIII, No.163, 1954, p. 7.
60. Greene, Graham, *The Man Within,* pp. 205-6.
61. Jones, William, *The Varieties of Religious Experience,* Mentor, New York, 1958, p. 142.
62. Greene, Graham, *The Comedians,* The Bodley Head, London, 1966, p. 72.
63. Browning, Robert, "Bishop Blougram's Apology," quoted by Graham Greene in *A Sort of Life*, p. 85.

Hell in Infancy

> *In the land of sky-scrapers, of stone stairs and cracked bells ringing early, one was aware of fear and hate, a kind of lawlessness—appalling cruelties could be practised without a second thought; one met for the first time characters, adult and adolescent, who bore about them the genuine quality of evil. There was Collifax who practised torments with dividers. Mr. Cranden with three grim chins, a dusty gown, a kind of demoniac sensuality. From these heights evil declined towards Parlow, whose desk was filled with minute photographs—advertisements of art photos. Hell lay about them in their infancy.*[1]

In this passage from the Prologue to Greene's novel *The Lawless Roads*, we get a picture of Greene's school building and dormitory mates at Berkhamstead. The school was also his childhood home since his father was the headmaster and his apartment was adjacent to the school dormitories. It is a picture of hell with devilish characters—Collifax, Cranden and Parlow. The atmosphere is characterised by "lawlessness" and "appalling cruelties" and "a demoniac sensuality." It was this childhood hell which Greene projects into his novels. The dark foreboding and lurid colours that are used to paint his grim settings were borrowed from the earliest scenes of his life. Greene's landscapes, which go by the name of "Greeneland," rival Dante's "Inferno" in its horror, crime and squalor. Early medieval England, rife with smugglers in *The Man Within:* war-torn London in *The Ministry of Fear;* "the graceless, sinless chromium world" where the banal drives of materialism have thrown human values overboard in *England Made Me*, a world of seediness and squalor in *The Power and the Glory* and *The Journey Without Maps;* contemporary political scenes of kidnappings, assassinations and push-button warfare in *The Honorary Consul* and *The Third Man;* the lepresorie in *A Burnt-Out Case*—these are some examples of the hell called Greeneland which is projected from the writer's childhood world. The truth that Greene points out about Pinkie, the juvenile criminal in *Brighton Rock* very well applies to Pinkie's creator:

> A brain was capable only of what it could conceive, and it couldn't conceive what it had never experienced; his cells were formed of the cement play-ground, the dead fire and the dying man in the St. Pancras waiting room, his bed at Billy's and his parents' bed.[2]

Greene's brain cells or memory is filled with the dour pictures of his school— "stone stairs and cracked bells." So haunted is he by the sheer monotony and iniquity these objects signify that he uses them recurrently in his novels. Anthony Farrant and Minty in *England Made Me* remember the same aspects of their school whenever they recall school with revulsion.

Greene's sense of place—the view of this world as different circles of hell is similar to that of one of his characters, Drewitt, a shady Lawyer in *Brighton Rock* who quotes Doctor Faustus, "Why. This is Hell, nor am I out of it."

In childhood, one forms the view of the world that will colour one's attitude always. With a sudden sense of horror, Greene reflects about Tench, the dentist in *The Power and the Glory,* who is conditioned by the unhappiness of his Metroland birthplace:

> We should be thankful we cannot see the horrors and the degradations lying around our childhood, in cupboards and bookshelves everywhere.[3]

And this idea is reinforced by him in *The Lawless Roads:*

> People are made by places I thought.[4]

Thus his school, the part-hideous modern brick is the primary tone of colour he uses to paint his backgrounds. He gives a detailed picture of his school in his autobiography:

> . . . there existed in the same house such grim rooms as those I lived in now. Even the door by which I entered the house was a different one . . . though no servant would have endured the squalor we lived in. There was a schoolroom with ink-stained nibbled desks insufficiently warmed by one cast iron stove, a changing-room smelling of sweet and stale clothes, stone stairs, worn by generations of feet, leading to a dormitory divided by pitch-pine partitions that gave inadequate privacy—no moment of the night was free from noise, a cough, a snore, a fart. Years later when I read the sermon on hell in Joyce's 'Portrait of the Artist,' I recognized the land I had inhabited . . . some twelve years ago because I had started a novel about a school. I revisited the scene and found no change. I abandoned the novel—I couldn't bear mentally living again for several years in these surroundings. A leper colony in the Congo was preferable. . . .[5]

The passage brings out the extremely morbid and seedy impression Greene's school made on him. This was the first mould which is endlessly reproduced in his novels. We can illustrate this Greene landscape with a few examples since to describe all the settings of his novels would not only be repetitious, but a distasteful exercise for the mind to put up with.

Brighton Rock has slums like Nelson Place, Peacehaven's and Billy's Lodgings for its settings. There are continual flashes of seediness and squalor. Images pile up one on top of the other. For example, "flapping gutters," "glassless windows," "a rotting discoloured face," "the basin full of stale water,[6] "the rotten bannister"—a whole world of fetid, decaying, putrefying chaos signifying moral degeneracy. The stench which pervades everywhere—the smell of rotting fish in a shabby street, a passage stinking like a lavatory—all are recreations of Greene's malodorous school-building.

In *The Heart of the Matter*, the images of squalor recur. West Africa, with its British colony represented by the building of the law courts and police-stations is described by Greene with the same vehement repulsion. With an accuracy of phrase, Greene blends the physical with the abstract; smells are suggestive of moral decay:

> In the dark narrow passage behind, in the charge-room and the cells, Scobie could always detect the odour of human meanness and injustice—it was the smell of the zoo, of saw dust, excrement, ammonia, and lack of liberty. The place was scrubbed daily, but you could never eliminate the smell. Prisoners and policemen carried it in their clothing like cigarette smoke.[6]

It's a Battlefield has cinematographic flashes of shabby basement flats strewn with hair combings "as large as a baby's skull," rooms with stale air, brothels which grow like mushrooms, factories where girls work precariously between disfigurement and death. It was in Africa, that Greene reached the nadir of squalor. He writes:

> There seemed to be a seediness about the place you couldn't get to the same extent elsewhere, and seediness has a very deep appeal.[7]

Birds of prey like vultures, insects and animals are constantly used in Greene's scenarios as symbols of a decaying world, of spiritual vacuity. Psychologists would relate these scenes to Greene's early phobia of birds and insects, and I strongly feel there is a subconscious connection. George W. Kisker, a leading psychologist states:

> Phobias are so common among children that they have been called the normal neuroses of childhood. Fear of the dark, ghosts and goblins, cemetries, and bugs and animals is an everyday occurrence among children. . . . During this period of development children learn to have fears which may influence their behaviour for the rest of their lives.[8]

Greene recalls in his autobiography:

> There were terrors, too, of course, but they would have been terrors at any age. . . . I had inherited from my mother a blinding terror or birds and bats. Even today I loathe the touch of feathers, and I remember how one night at Harston a bat came into my bedroom. . . . I shrieked with my head under the sheet. . . . The fear of bats remains. I had to steel myself later in Angkor Wat to pass a damaged bat. . . .[9]

A bat is a symbol of omen in Greene's short story, "The End of the Party." Francis Morton dreams of a bat swooping over him. At the end of that day, Francis dies. *The Power and the Glory* opens with the scene of a vulture which reflects the chief atmosphere of the place—moral decay. West Africa breeds its ugly fauna in *The Heart of the Matter*—rats, cockroaches, flies, mosquitoes, vultures. In *It's a Battlefield,* dead bats lie on the floor in the basement flats. Liberia described in *Journey Without Maps,* teems with jigger and rodents that nibble off people's feet.

Many places in Greeneland like war-torn London in *The Ministry of Fear* and war-ravaged Vietnam in *The Quiet American,* are filled with the lurid glow of gun-fire and napalm bombs. One may go to the extent of connecting early fears with a writer's later creativity. Greene's consciousness, on his own admission is so much formed on childhood terrors which he describes in *A Sort of Life.* We see a subconscious link between the scenes of fire in his novels with his early "pyrophobia"—or pathological fear of fire around him. He writes:

> Another recurring terror was of the house catching fire at night. . . . There always seemed to be fires in those days and yet I never actually saw a fire until I witnessed too many of them in the winter of 1940-41.[10]

In *The Confidential Agent,* Greene describes the London blitz:

> Nearer and nearer the guns opened up, but the plane pursued its steady terror. . . . But the bomb burst half a mile away: you could feel the ground dent.[11]

And again in *The Quiet American:*

> . . . one burst only was required, there was no one to return our fire.[12]

In Greeneland, the foreboding sense of violence and death hovers over the scene. So much so that Fowler, the journalist in *The Quiet American,* reporting the Vietnam war scene, calls Death the fourth major character of the novel. Greene seemed to have a penchant for the macabre and as a child he noticed the atmosphere of terror hovering over a part of his home-town. He describes it in his autobiography:

> At the far end of the long High Street was the village of Northchurch and an old inn, the Crooked Billet. The name . . . always had for me a sinister ring (in the inn I was sure travellers had been done to death) and this gave the whole Northchurch village an atmosphere of standing outside the pale: a region of danger where nightmare might easily become reality.[13]

Greeneland is a transmogrification of the region of danger where nightmare might easily become reality. Thus Haiti of *The Comedians* is described as "The Nightmare Republic" ("mpossible to deepen that night"). Brighton of *Brighton Rock* with razor-slashing criminals stands "outside the pale."

Greene's first memory of the scene of death is that of a dog lying dead under his pram:

> . . . my mother once told me how surprised she had been months later by some reference which I made to the 'poor dog.' They were almost the first words I had spoken.[14]

Another memory Greene recalls in his autobiography is of a man who ran into a house near the Grand Junction Canal to cut his throat.

To the fear of death is added the fear of drowning which Greene developed during an early attack of pleurisy:

> I was able to imagine my lungs filling with water.[15]

The pain he got from a dental extraction left him sensitive to pain:

> Till now I have never suffered greater pain than I did then. I remember rolling on the drawing room floor in agony from an exposed nerve.[16]

In Greeneland a dentist is a symbol of painful experiences. For example Mr. Tench of *The Power and the Glory* and the self-conscious, insensitive Victor Rhodes in *The Complaisant Lover.*

The sight of blood during an operation to remove Greene's adenoids left him so frightened that

> . . . for thirty years after that . . . blood worried and sickened me, so that sometimes I fainted at the mere description of an accident.[17]

Greene recalls, too, that he was menaced by the fear of a witch "who would lurk at night on the nursery landing."

All these early experiences blend in Greene's consciousness

to emerge in his novels as a terrifying force. Death, violence and brutality pervade his scenarios. Greene reflects about his character "D." in *The Confidential Agent:*

> . . . if he had found himself on a desert island, he would have expected to infect even the loneliness somehow with violence.[18]

The words, obviously show Greene's self-estimate. Greene's scenes are by and large descriptions of death and violence.

In fact, there is something primitive in the world's violence and cruelty. To Greene, it is traceable not only to his own vision of the world as a child, but existed in the racial childhood of man. It dwells in the central darkness. Greene says in *The Journey Without Maps:*

> Today our world seems peculiarly susceptible to brutality. There is a touch of nostalgia in the pleasure we take in gangster novels, in characters who have so agreeably simplified their emotions that they have begun living again at a level below the cerebral. We, like Wordsworth, are living after a war and a revolution, and these half-castes fighting with bombs between the cliffs of skyscrapers seem more likely than we to be aware of Proteus rising from the sea. It is not, of course, that one wishes to stay forever at that level, but when one sees to what unhappiness, to what peril of extinction centuries of cerebration have brought us, one sometimes has a curiosity to discover if one can from what we have come, to recall at which point we went astray.[19]

Brighton Rock opens in such a way that we are immediately drawn into a world of violence:

> Hale knew, before he had been in Brighton three hours that they meant to murder him. . . .[20]

One feels at the end of the novel that one had been cut by the Boy's razor blades and as if an excruciating pain had followed. Like Macbeth, the Boy thinks it necessary to commit one murder to cover up an earlier one and so a series of murders takes place. And at the end blinded by his own vitriol, he jumps a precipice to his own death.

Willi Hilfe in *The Ministry of Fear* highlights the ethos of the modern world:

> But all the same you have to be prepared in these days for criminals—everywhere. They call it having ideals. They'll even talk about murder being the most merciful thing.[21]

And in the same novel it is stated the allies of the Nazis "do not see blood like you and me. . . . It's all statistics to them."[22]

The Confidential Agent opens with scenes of death hovering over the scene:

> The gulls swept over Dover. They sailed out like flakes of the fog, and tacked back towards the hidden town, while the siren mourned with them: other ships replied, a whole wake lifted up their voices—for whose death?[23]

Modern war and international intrigue are the mis-in-scene for Greene's contemporary novels. *A Gun for Sale* was suggested by the nefarious activities and alliances of armament manufacturers; *The Confidential Agent* by the Spanish Civil War. *The Ministry of Fear* by Nazi Fifth Column activities in Britain; *The Third Man* by the penicillin racket in post-war Viennia; *Our Man in Havana* by Big Power intrigues in Cuba. Saavedra, the writer in *The Honorary Consul*, sums up the subject matter of contemporary novels. It may be a statement about Greene's own novels:

> Assassinations, kidnappings, the torture of prisoners.[24]

Greene's school system is the prototype of the sense of injustice, moral corruption, loneliness and spiritual vacancy that broods over the scenes of his novels. The epigraph of *It's a Battlefield* contains a passage from Kinglake's "Eothen." The world is a battlefield made of small numberless circlets in which each separate battalion is fighting its own battle in happy ignorance of the general aim of the battle. In the same novel, Conder delineates the force called human justice:

> The world, he thought . . . was run by the whims of a few men, the whims of a politician, a journalist and a policeman. They hanged this man and pardoned that; one embezzler was in prison, but the other men of the same sort were sent to Parliament.[25]

The blocks of prison marked A, B, C in the same novel, remind one of the circles of Dante's hell. Loneliness pervades the basement flats:

> Loneliness was only too easily attained; it was in the air one breathed; open any door, it opened on the loneliness in the passage.[26]

Similarly, Scobie describes the general moral decrepitude in West Africa in *The Heart of the Matter:*

> Heaven remained rigidly in its proper place on the other side of death, and on this side flourished the injustices, the cruelties, the meanness that elsewhere people so cleverly hushed up.[27]

One of the best recreations of the utter spiritual vacancy characterizing Greene's School is the sanatorium in *The Ministry of Fear* where Rowe is confined, afflicted with amnesia. It is a picture of efficiency without love. The apparent aim of the sanatorium is health but it is only clinical health that is devoid of charity. The wing of the sanatorium euphemistically called the Sick Bay has an unhappy brooding purpose. To Rowe it seems:

> the conception of Hell presented by sympathetic theologians—a place without inhabitants which existed simply as a warning.[28]

Greene's school was a "sick bay" where the apparent purpose was inculcation of knowledge, but it was devoid of love and purpose.

The passage quoted in the beginning also brings into focus another aspect of Greene's concept of hell. Hell is where evil flourishes, where demoniac characters like Parlow, Crandon and Collifax practice tortures on the others. In Greene's novels, "evil walks in triumph" and "goodness does not pay." This concept of hell, first became manifest to Greene in his reading of Marjorie Bowen's novel, *The Viper of Milan.* The villainous Visconti Mastino della Scala helped to explain "the terrible living world of the stone stairs and the never quiet dormitory" where Parlow and Crandon practised tortures with dividers. Greene explains the victory of evil portrayed in the book:

> It was no good in that real world to dream that one would ever be a Sir Henry Curtis, but della Scala who at last turned from an honesty that never paid and betrayed his friends and died dishonoured and a failure even in treachery—it was easier for a child to escape behind that mask.[29]

The earliest faces Greene saw in his home-town were:

> those curious individual faces which I feel I could recognize now anywhere in the world: painted faces like the knaves on playing cards, with a slyness about the eyes, an unsuccessful cunning.[30]

In Greene's novels, we see those sly, cunning people in characters like Yusef of *The Heart of the Matter,* Pinkie of *Brighton Rock,* Harry Lime of *The Third Man.*

Evil is so pervasive in Greeneland that it seems Greene, like the whiskey-priest in *The Power and the Glory:*

> carried Hell about with him. . . . Evil ran like malaria in his veins.[31]

We may aptly sum up by a remark made by Greene about his earliest realization:

> Goodness has only once found a perfect incarnation and never will again, but evil can always find a home there. Human nature is not black and white but black and grey. I read all that in 'The Viper and Milan' and I looked round and saw that it was so.[32]

NOTES

1. Greene, Graham, *The Lawless Roads*, Heinemann, London, 1955, p. 10.
2. Greene, Graham, *Brighton Rock,* Heinemann, London, 1955, p. 306
3. Greene, Graham, *The Power and the Glory,* Heinemann, London, 1940.
4. Greene, Graham, *The Lawless Roads*, p. 10.
5. Greene, Graham, *A Sort of Life,* Penguin, London, 1971, p. 54.
6. Greene, Graham, *The Heart of the Matter,* The Reprint Society, London, 1950. pp. 5-6.
7. Greene, Graham, *The Journey Without Maps,* Heinemann, London, 1940, pp. 7-8.
8. Kisker, George W., *The Disorganized Personality,* McGraw Hill, Kogakusha, Tokyo, p. 198.

9. Greene, Graham, *A Sort of Life*, pp. 23-24.
10. Ibid., p. 24.
11. Greene, Graham, *The Confidential Agent*, Heinemann, London, 1956, p 21
12. Greene, Graham, *The Quiet American*, Heinemann, London, 1960, p. 195.
13. Greene, Graham, *A Sort of Life*, p. 12
14. Ibid., p. 13.
15. Ibid., p. 28.
16. Ibid., p. 15.
17. Ibid.
18. Greene, Graham, *The Confidential Agent*, p. 44.
19. Greene, Graham, *The Journey Without Maps*, p. 10.
20. Greene, Graham, *Brighton Rock*, p. 1.
21. Greene, Graham, *The Ministry of Fear*, Heinemann, London, 1960, p. 34.
22. Ibid., p. 50.
23. Greene, Graham, *The Confidential Agent*, p. 9.
24. Greene, Graham, *The Honorary Consul*, Penguin, London, 1964.
25. Greene, Graham, *It's a Battlefield*, Heinemann, London, 1956, pp. 38-39.
26. Ibid., p. 217.
27. Greene, Graham, *The Heart of the Matter*.
28. Greene, Graham, *The Ministry of Fear*, p. 30.
29. Greene, Graham, "The Lost Childhood" in *Collected Essays*.
30. Greene, Graham, *A Sort of Life*, p. 11
31. Greene, Graham, *The Power and the Glory*, p. 89.
32. Greene, Graham, "The Lost Childhood" in *Collected Essays*, p. 16.

The Spot of Decay: Dangerous Innocence

> *The world was in her heart already,*
> *like a small spot of decay in the fruit.*[1]

Greene's early life and those of his characters was to have a negative repercussion on their later lives. This experience has become a warning to society and man in general in Greene's works that childhood must not be taken for granted, that the innocence of children is easily susceptible to the corruption of adults lurking around, that the slightest stain in a child's character could spread into unrecognizable size in later life and that if the adults did not take care to protect the happiness and sanctity of children, it would have dire consequences for mankind.

The quotation at the beginning of this chapter applies to Brigitta, the illegitimate daughter of the Whiskey Priest in *The Power and the Glory*, but it may be related to a host of child characters in Greene's works. All these characters are frighteningly mature in their awareness of evil so early in life. They have been

> rushed through a saturnalia of adult passions and attitudes.[2]

We feel there is nothing they do not know, little they do not understand. Thus Brigitta in *The Power and the Glory*, leers enticingly, has the brash confidence of the adolescent who has ripened too quickly. "She was her father's sin made living and whole."[3]

The adolescent, Else, in *The Confidential Agent* makes D, the agent, reflect:

> Fourteen was a dreadfully early age at which to know so much and be so powerless.[4]

And again:

> You learned too much in these days before you came of age.[5]

Anna Hilfe in *The Ministry of Fear* is described as very small and thin and looks too young for all the things she must have seen.

All these child characters never seem to have had a childhood in so far as innocence is concerned and they are incarnations of the boys and girls Greene saw in his home-town, Berkhamstead, and whom he describes in the prologue to his *Lawless Roads*. The evocative phrases sum up a world in which the corruption of adults has completely infected the very young:

> Sexual experience came to them too early, too easily. Youths "with smeared and scented hair and bitten cigarettes" greeting girls with "careless roughness"; the "shabby little shops selling second—hand copies of London life—articles about high heels and long hair," a young girl kneeling in the damp "with an expression abased and secretive whilst she sawed through the limbs of a bush"; a boy and a girl who were found headless on the railway line. The girl was expecting her second child. Her first had been born when she was thirteen, and . . . her parents had been unable to fix responsibility among fourteen youths.[6]

The imagery goes on piling bringing out Greene's horror of a childhood that was lost all too quickly.

In his short story. "The Destructors," Greene brings into focus the enfant terrible, the child who has never known innocence. A gang of boys, led by a boy whose father was an architect, systematically destroys a beautiful house left standing after a blitz. The boys, in fact, complete what the war could not finish. An inverted image evokes the frightening lack of childhood innocence:

> The grey ash floated above them and fell on their heads like age.[7]

William Wordsworth has said about grown-ups: "The world is too much with us." Greene says the same thing about children. The world has completely possessed many unfortunate children. The little boy in Greene's short story "The Hint of an Explanation" chooses a toy that reflects the ugly intrusion of modern existence into early life. Gazing on the electric train, he says:

> The tears of longing came into my eyes when I looked at the turntable. It was my favourite piece—it looked so ugly and practical and true.[8]

The words "ugly," "practical and true" sum up the modern child's earliest tastes. They show the influence of an adult, mechanized life.

The child is separated from the adult by an enormous gulf that differentiates their vision. The innocent have a glorious vision in which everything is permeated with bliss. This is the theme of William Wordsworth's poem, Ode to Childhood:

> There was a time when meadow,grove and stream,
> The earth, and every common sight,
> To me did seem,
> Apparell'd in celestial light.[9]

And again the poet states:

> Heaven lies about us inout infancy![10]

Greene presents the same theme in three short stories: "I Spy," "The Innocent" and "The Blue Film."

In "I Spy," a boy creeps downstairs at night to his father's tobacco shop to smoke his first cigarette. He is surprised to see his father with two strangers. From his hiding-place, the boy overhears them talking. The boy can understand nothing of their talk, but it is clear to him that his father is leaving and the strangers have some influence over him. We suspect that the men are policemen, but know nothing more. The great difference between us and the boy is that we are aware that some such things do happen in an adult world of crime. But for the boy, it appears strange, almost an exercise in magic. His knowledge does not include as yet, the subject of corruption.

In "The Innocent," a man takes a tart to his childhood home for the night. Overcome by the nostalgic smell of innocence the place evokes, he sneaks out in the dark to look at a house where he used to take dancing lessons. He had once loved a little girl there, but she had paid no attention to him. He remembers how he had left messages filled with an innocent passion for her in a hole in the gatepost. He finds one still there. It contains what appears to him now to be an obscene drawing. But, as a child:

> he had believed, he was drawing something with a meaning unique and beautiful; it was only now after thirty years of life that the picture seemed obscene.[11]

A similar idea—the difference of vision in a child and in an adult—is dealt with in Greene's story, "The Blue Film." Here he describes the tender, pure feelings experienced by a man who watches a blue film in which he himself had once taken part. To us, with an adult imagination, the film might appear vulgar. For him, it was related to a period of innocence and therefore evoked no revulsion.

Related to Greene's idea of the innocent vision, is the theme of adult intrusion into the child's world. A tenuous line separates the child from the corrupt world of adults. The child stands very vulnerably near the wickedness of grown-up man. The adults may wrongly believe that children are ignorant of everything corrupt, but the terrible truth is that the child understands and senses with some in-built power. A wrong action by adults in the presence of a child may prove the beginning of the child's corruption. His impressionable mind may soon multiply the evil he sees and his blissful childhood is over all too soon. Greene treats this theme in his story "The Basement Room." Philip Lane, a boy of seven finds himself between two servants in his large Belgravia House, when his parents go off for a holiday. Free of parental restraints, he sets foot for the first time on the stairs leading to the basement of his house. The basement may signify the world of adult goings-on. Adult corruption impinges on his senses. He is apprehensive of new realities:

> All his seven nursery years vibrated with the strange, the new experience.[12]

There is a strained relationship between the two servants—Mr. and Mrs. Baines. This is because Mr. Baines is having an adulterous affair with a girl. Philip Lane, cannot fully comprehend the situation but he can sense an unhappy feeling pervading the house:

> . . . a strange passion he couldn't understand moving in the basement room.[13]

On a walk, Philip sees his butler, Baines with a girl in a shop. Their manner is enough to suggest an affair of corruption. It snatches away his blissful innocence and conditions him for life:

> . . . he was less sheltered than he had ever been; other people's lives for the first time touched and pressed and moulded. He would never escape that scene. In a week he had forgotten it, but it conditioned his career, the long austerity of his life; when he was dying he said, 'Who is she.'[14]

Baines asks Philip to keep the affair a secret from Mrs. Baines, but at an unguarded moment, he spills it out. It makes him feel miserable.

. . . grown-up people should keep their own secrets.[15]

The impact of the adult affair is life-long on the child. It withers him before he can even bloom. Mrs. Baines tempts him with a Meccano set if he does not tell Mr. Baines that she knows the secret.

> A 2 A, Meccano set, Master Philip. He never opened his Meccano set again, never built anything, died, the old dilettante, sixty years later with nothing.[16]

Greene's dictum is further revealed in these words:

> Let grown-up people keep to their world and he would keep to his, safe in the small garden between the plane-trees. 'In the lost childhood of Judas, Christ was betrayed'; you could almost see the small unformed face hardening into the deep dilettante selfishness of age.[17]

A similar theme is developed in Greene's novel *The Human Factor*. The world of modern warfare and violence has invaded today's child. Parents, anxious to protect their children from their own miserable corruption, like Greene, fail to do so. The hero of *The Human Factor* is described talking to his son Sam. The man, called Castle is white himself but his wife is black. His son Sam too is black. Standing at Berkhamstead Common (Greene's own favourite childhood haunt) Castle talks to his son:

> 'Did they shoot spies there?'
> 'No. No. What gave you that idea? . . . .'
> 'But there are spies, aren't there—real spies?'
> 'I suppose so, yes, why do you ask?

The child continues:

> 'What's a dragon?'

'You know—one of those armoured creatures spitting out fire.'
'Like a tank?'
'Well, yes, I suppose like a tank.'
There was a lack of contact between their two imaginations.[18]

The conversation between two generations shows the difference of concerns. While the father talks about dragons, the son's imagination is peopled with spies and tanks—symbols of twentieth century life. Castle reads a poem to his son—a poem that contains childhood associations for him since he read it himself as a child. Sam is interested in a part of the poem, which the father himself does not consider important. It concerns a highwayman. Violence has already broken into the child's world:

'That's the one. That's the one I like best.'
'It's a bit frightening' Castle said.
'That's why I like it . . .'
'Has he a white face like you and Mr. Muller?'
'It doesn't say'
'I think he's black, black as my hat, black as my cat.'
'Why.'
'I think all the white people are afraid of him and lock their house, in case he comes in with a carving knife and cuts their throats slowly,' he added with relish.

Sam had never looked more black, Castle thought. He put his arm round his with a gesture of protection, but he couldn't protect him from the violence and vengeance which were beginning to work in the child's heart.[19]

The implications of the corruption of children by adults or the world around are grave. And in a series of children stories, Greene tries to tell children that they must keep away from adults and their rottenness. These books, illustrated by Dorothy Craigie have a vehicle as a hero. Thus the books are *The Little Horse Bus, The Little Steam-roller, The Little Fire-Engine, The Little Train*. In these stories, a despised vehicle performs a noteworthy, fantastic task. It takes the side of the law against a criminal. It becomes a hunter. The alienation and pursuit features are autobiographical. Greene experienced them himself at school. The only difference between the vehicles anr Greene is that while the vehicles are hunters, Greene was the hunted in early life. When the Little Train dreams of a visit to the world outside where the great expresses go, he gets into bad straits. He finds the outside world ugly and noisy and a Scotch express pushes him home. In *The Little Horse Bus* mention is made of a trunk labelled "Brighton-on-Sea," which is a weak reference to the world of Pinkie, the juvenile killer. The shadow of evil is not far away from the world of children. Kenneth Allot and Miriam Farris state that Greene's utopia for children remains frustrated:

> Greene goes along with innumerable poets and other writers in accepting a golden age of innocence in the earliest years, but what he stresses is how soon it is threatened by evil in childhood.[20]

Wordsworth was to lament the same loss of the visionary gleam of infancy:

> Shades of the prison-house begin to close
> Upon the growing Boy.[21]

Throughout his works, Greene shows himself as the champion of the children's right to their happiness and innocence. Greene wrote a scurrilous article in *Night and Day,* a magazine, in October 1937, against Twentieth Century Fox, a film company, for "procuring" the child artist, Miss Shirley Temple "for immoral purposes" for their film "Wee Willie Winkie." Greene

> suggested that she had a certain adroit coquetry which appealed to middle-aged men.[22]

The article caused a furore and the film company filed a case of libel against the magazine. Greene recalls the intense reaction the counsel had to his article:

> it was such a beastly libel to have written that if it had been a question of money it would be difficult to say what would be an appropriate amount to arrive at.[23]

Greene further says that the magazine had to cease publication and apologies had to be made on Greene's behalf by the magazine company. I am inclined to say, being the staunch advocate of children's innocence, Greene himself would not have subscribed to the apologies.

Greene voices his opinion against the killing of innocents in war in *The Quiet American* with intense loathing for war. He describes Fowler's reactions (his, too) to a scene in the Vietnam war. (Fowler is a reporter):

> They were very clearly dead: a small neat clot of blood on the woman's forehead, and the child might have been sleeping. He was about six years old and he lay like an embryo in the womb with his little bony knees drawn up. . . . There was a gnawed piece of loaf under his body. I thought, 'I hate war.'[24]

Greene cannot reconcile, like Scobie in *The Heart of the Matter*, the love of God with the suffering of children, who have not bargained for it. Reflecting on Helen Rolt who has survived a shipwreck, Greene writes:

> It would need all Father Brule's ingenuity to explain that. Not that the child would die—that needed no explanation. Even the pagans realized that the love of God might mean an early death, though the reason ascribed was different; but that the child should have been allowed to survive the forty days and nights in the open boat—that was the mystery, to reconcile that with the love of God.[25]

Everywhere in Greene's world children grow up crippled spiritually because of many reasons for which the adults are to blame. And, I may add, these children in turn spoil others when they grow up. So the chain goes on and the world becomes gloomier.

When children grow up without maturing, they are an unmitigated danger to themselves and to society. To live in an adult world, children need a ripe imagination. Being stunted psychologically, the grown-up innocents provoke dangers. For example, Anthony Farrant in *England Made Me* is an innocent grown-up in Krogh's world of big money and crime. He is innocent of the implications of working for evil men like Krogh for whom human values are exchangeable for money. The result is, he foolishly contradicts Krogh and sides with dismissed workers and, therefore, is killed. Alden Pyle, in *The Quiet American* is a dangerous innocent. He bases his idealism of salvation for Vietnam on books and avowed to the ideal he goes about killing innocent people. His innocence lies in his incapacity to distinguish between idealism and reality.

Harry Lime in *The Third Man,* the cheerful rascal of school days—turns into a ruthless criminal, blind to all human values. He is engaged in the penicillin adulteration racket. Human lives are expendable for easy money—free of income-tax. His case is that of the person who has not grown up in a moral sense, whose innocence is itself dragged into a wickedness. Lime's friend, Rollo Martin thinks:

> He's never grown-up. Marlowe's devils wore squibs attached to their tails. Evil was like Peter Pan. It carried with it the horrifying and horrible gift of eternal youth.[26]

Greene's attitude to children is one of father-like concern. What Connor Cruise O'Brien remarks about Scobie in *The Heart of the Matter* applies to Greene:

> This solitary tentacle of his takes hold only on children, or on adults who appear to him in the guise of children. . . . The

people who touch him must be immature and helpless: he alone is responsible, the policeman, the father.[27]

NOTES

1. Greene, Graham, *The Power and the Glory*, Heinemann, London, 1940, p. 62.
2. Atkins, John, *Graham Greene,* Calder Boyars, London, 1957, p. 120.
3. Ibid.
4. Greene, Graham, *The Confidential Agent*, Heinemann, London, 1959, p. 39.
5. Ibid., p. 50.
6. Greene, Graham, *The Lawless Roads*, Heinemann, London, 1955, p. 6.
7. Greene, Graham, "The Destructors," in *Twenty One Stories*, Heinemann, London, 1954, p. 54.
8. Greene, Graham, "The Hint of an Explanation," in *Twenty One Stories*, p. 42.
9. Wordsworth, William, "Ode on Intimations of Immortality from Recollections of Early Childhood," *The Golden Treasury*, Bk. IV, ed. Francis Turner Palgrave, Oxford Univ. Press, London, 1959, pp. 136-37.
10. Ibid., p. 137.
11. Greene, Graham, "The Innocent" in *Nineteen Stories*, Lion Books, New York, 1949, p. 32.
12. Greene, Graham, "The Basement Room," *Modern English Short Stories*, selected by Derek Hudson, Oxford Univ. Press, Delhi, 1977, p. 129.
13. Ibid., p. 10.
14. Ibid., p. 136.
15. Ibid., p. 140.
16. Ibid., p. 141.
17. Ibid., p. 150.

18. Greene, Graham, *The Human Factor,* The Bodley Head, London, 1980, pp. 69-70.
19. Ibid., p. 186.
20. Allot, Kenneth and Miriam Farris, The Art of Graham Greene, Hamish Hamilton, London, 1951, p. 25.
21. Wordsworth, William, "Ode on Intimations to Immortality . . .," p. 137.
22. Greene, Graham, *Ways of Escape,* The Bodley Head, London, 1980, p. 72.
23. Ibid.
24. Greene, Graham, *The Quiet American,* Heinemann, London (Uniform ed.), 1960, pp. 62-63.
25. Greene, Graham, *The Heart of the Matter,* The Reprint Society, London, 1950, p. 114.
26. Greene, Graham, *The Third Man,* Heinemann, London, 1958, pp. 128-29.
27. O'Brien, Connor Cruise, *Maria Cross: Imaginative Patterns in Group of Modern Catholic Writers,* Burns and Oates, London, 1959, pp. 78-9.

The Burden of Childhood: Greene and Other Writers

> *There are certain writers, as different as Dickens from Kipling, who never shake off the burden of their childhood. . . . All later experience seems to have been related to those months or years of unhappiness.*[1]

What Greene says about other writers in the passage above, applies to himself too. In previous chapters we have seen how Greene's works are an attempt to recreate the world of his childhood—"those months or years of unhappiness," which resulted in his morbid sense of evil, his attraction for failure, the duality of vision that characterises his theology and political ideology and the sense of guilt and frustration attached to his vision of human love. In this chapter we may compare and contrast the impact of Greene's childhood on his adult life with the experience of other writers, some of whom were his contemporaries and others who lived before him. Since the "zeitgeist" or soul of the times influences a number of writers in a common way, a similarity may be seen in their works. And since each writer is yet an individual with unique reactions to life, differences in perception are bound to exist. Thus we may study Greene's reactions to childhood sufferings, his awareness of evil and death, the influence of books read early in his life, the influence of his school on his later life—all in comparison to the experiences of Charles Dickens, Rudyard Kipling, H.H. Munro, Henry James, Jean-Paul Sartre, W.H. Auden, and George Orwell. They all share the common "burden of childhood."

The first aspect of this comparative study deals with the nature of suffering in early life and the reactions of the different writers as gleaned in their works. Greene's sufferings as a child have already been described in an earlier chapter "In the Lost Boyhood of Judas." What we notice about his suffering is the fact, that it emanated more from his own peculiar, morbid temperament than from external circumstances in his family or immediate surroundings. Peter Quennell, his schoolfellow describes the different ways in which he (Quennell) and Greene reacted to the same school.

> The school that we both attended proved to have been a place of almost unfathomable iniquity. . . . But I was conscious neither of the hellish atmosphere of the pedestrian life I lived at school, nor the signs of spiritual degeneracy that I might have run to earth among the adjacent streets . . . the intimations of evil that seem to have coloured Greene's youth, and that since then have had so profound an effect on the shaping of his creative talents, failed somehow to enrich mine.[2]

From Quennell's description it appears that Greene was temperamentally inclined to notice the pessimistic side of things. There are incidents of crime as well as those of goodness taking place all around children wherever and whenever they have existed. But some children notice only the things that appear right. In fact, most children interpret things around them in the innocent light of early vision. Some exceptional ones, like Greene, wear dark glasses even in childhood and the accent in their vision falls on the morbid, macabre aspects of life. What I am trying to maintain is that Greene's suffering was not caused or provoked by intensely unhappy circumstances like in the case of other writers. His school might have been a cause for unhappiness, but it was primarily Greene's mind which interpreted it like that which provokes a sense of terrible aboriginal calamity that infects his novels.

Greene in his essay, "The Burden of Childhood" notes the tragedy of unhappy circumstances that ruined the childhood of three writers:

> The abandonment to the blacking factory in Dickens' case and in Kipling's to the cruel Aunt Rosa living in the sandy suburban road were never forgotten. . . . Life which turns its cruel side to most of us at an age when we have begun to learn the arts of self-protection took these two writers by surprise during the defenselessness of early childhood.[3]

With Charles Dickens, fate contrived the worst to make him a lonely, unhappy child. His father suffered from grave financial troubles. Unable to pay off debts, he was removed to Marshalsea Debtors' Prison where later his mother and other members of the family joined in. Dickens had to slog at the horrible blacking factory which is recreated as Murdstone and Grinby in his book, *David Copperfield.* His plight was terrible as described by Angus Wilson:

> He found himself an abandoned small boy, ill-lodged, underfed, often aimlessly wandering the streets—'no advice, no counsel, no encouragement,' . . . and it all happened in a horrible flash of time.[4]

Greene tells us in his essay "The Burden of Childhood" that Kipling and H.H. Munro suffered for similar reasons. They were children of colonial civil servants who were usually away from home for long periods of duty. Both, therefore, lacked parental love. Besides, they were left to the guardianship of aunts who proved very wicked and cruel to their wards. Kipling sets down the suffering of that period in his story *Baa Baa Black Sheep* reliving the beatings at the hands of Aunt Rosa, the humiliation of having a card with "liar" written on it pinned to his back and his neglected growing blindness. Munro's Aunt Augusta was a woman of ungovernable temper and was

> quite capable of making a child's life miserable.[5]

She chose Munro's younger brother for the beatings which provoked a sense of injustice in Munro.

While all the three writers suffered in one way or the other, they reacted differently to similar situations. Their writings show different repercussions. Dickens learnt sympathy.

> He developed a style so easy and natural that it seems to be capable of including the human race in its understanding.[6]

But Kipling and Munro reacted with anger. Hatred of different degrees motivate and sustained their creative talents.

> Kipling designed a machine, the cogwheels perfectly fashioned for exclusion.[7]

Revenge is Kipling's chief humour and with Munro it is the desire to make the reader aware of injustice.

To elaborate a little with illustrations the reactions of these writers we must peep into some of their works. Dickens despite great childhood suffering, throws off the bitterness of the past and recounts his childhood with tints of humour. When he revisited Marshalsea Prison in later life to recall the atmosphere of the place where his father was imprisoned (he wanted to use it for his book *Little Dorrit),* he was not overwhelmed by associations of grief. Angus Wilson writes:

> Despite the ruined state of the now defunct prison he located a room peculiarly nostalgic to him because it had been the room of a drunken Captain Porter whom he had immortalized in *David Copperfield.* He asked a small boy in the street: 'Who lives there?' and was answered, 'Jack Pithick.' 'Who is Jack Pithick?' he asked him. And the answer was 'Joe Pithick's Uncle.' I quote this because in describing the traumatic effect of these boyhood months on Dickens, it is easy to suggest a man deeply buried in his past. Nothing could be further from the truth. . . . Indeed his delight at the boy's answer may be seen as a send-up of his own concern with buried sorrows.[8]

There is yet another way in which Dickens reacted to those early years. Suffering gave him the power to understand and sympathise with the plight of the downtrodden. Angus Wilson expresses a similar view:

> . . . the misery of those abandoned months, the suppressed panic, the shame and loneliness bit so deeply into him that only Dostoevsky, Gissing and Jack London among novelists have equalled his absolute power of identification with the outcaste.[9]

To show the contrast with Dickens, we may quote Kipling's *Baa Baa Black Sheep.*

> 'If you make me do that,' said Black Sheep very quietly. 'I shall burn this house down and perhaps I will kill you. I don't know whether I can kill you—you are so bony, but I will try.'
>
> No punishment followed this blasphemy, though Black Sheep held himself ready to work his way to Auntie Rosa's withered throat and grip there till he was beaten off.[10]

The feeling of bitter hatred is unmistakable in the lines above. Pure revenge seems to be Kipling's motivating force. As Greene says, "Aunt Rosa had established herself in the mind of her victim and corrupted it."

Although a tone of outrage is discernible in Munro's works, it is more out of a desire to bring injustice to light, than to wreak revenge. We can measure the hatred he felt for Aunt Augusta in his book *Sredni Vashtar* where Conradin, the small boy prays successfully for vengeance on his tame ferret.

Greene's own reactions to childhood misery is nearer Munro's than Kipling's and Dicken's. Kipling is too revengeful compared with Greene, and Dickens too generous and forgiving. Greene has had his tormentors, one named Carter, who has been discussed earlier. He had established himself in Greene's consciousness since school-days. Greene identifies him with the villain

Mastino della Scala, in the *Viper of Milan*—the prototype of evil characters in Greene's works. In Greene's books, the hero is hunted and tormented and often the hunted turns on his chaser and runs him down. The name Carter is given to a number of bad characters in his works—like in *The Bear Fell Free* and *Our Man in Havana*. But on the whole Greene's stance is nearer to Munro's—to reveal the working of injustice and to commend just punishment for it.

Jean-Paul Sartre, the French existentialist-philosopher whose prolific out-put radically influenced the thinking of the twentieth century, won the Nobel Prize for his autobiography, *Words*. The sub-title of this book is suggestive of all his suffering as a child—*I loathe my childhood and all that remains of it*. The present (the time he was writing) is evidence of deep childhood impressions. Sartre's autobiography reveals that his suffering was related to his father's death a little after his own birth, and the misery of his widowed mother who was despised by the rest of the family. Like Greene, Sartre's philosophical turn of mind must have contributed to his morbid reactions to his early sorrows. He did not lack the warmth of love for his mother was very affectionate to him and he was idolised by his grandfather who pampered him. But a note of despair is heard in his reflections on his father who left the world too soon to give his son the pleasure of his company. Was there a buried love then? Was there an unrequited desire for a father's love in his heart? At least one can feel these things in Sartre's words:

> The rule is that there are no good fathers; it is not the men who are at fault, but the paternal bond which is rotten.... If he had lived, my father would have lain down on me and crushed me. Fortunately, he died young.... I left behind me a dead young man who did not have the time to be my father, and could, today be my son. Was it a good or a bad thing? I do not know; but I am happy to subscribe to the judgement of an eminent psychoanalyst: I have no Superego.[11]

Without drawing too close a parallel with Greene, I would say that Greene's autobiography, *A Sort of Life,* indicates that his relation to his father was at best indifferent. He mentions here that his mother held his full respect, but that he always wondered why a man like his father should take any interest at all in the doings of a child. Only later, on his father's death did Greene discover a buried love for him which surfaced in dreams. No strong parallel can be drawn between Sartre's and Greene's attitude to their fathers, but in Greene's works there are characters who despise their fathers. Thus in *England Made Me*, Anthony Farrant is described as a failure resulting from his father's over-enthusiastic designs to mould him as a child. Andrews in *The Man Within*, strongly hates his father and considers him to be one great factor for the ruination of his character. Raven, in *The Gun for Sale*, strikes a similarly patriphobic note. He considers his harelip an inheritance that damns him. His parents could not afford a skilful surgeon to rectify the deformity. He reflects:

> Three minutes in bed or against a wall and then a lifetime for the one that's born.[12]

This reaction reminds one of Sartre's reflection on his father:

> I was lucky to belong to a dead man: a dead man had poured out the few drops of sperm which are the normal price of a child.[13]

Now we must turn to another aspect of Sartre where comparison may be drawn with Greene. The influence of early reading has been profound in the shaping of the attitudes of these writers. They both acknowledge this in their autobiographies and in other works. Greene writes in his autobiography:

> The influence of early books is profound. So much of the future lies on the shelves: early reading has more influence on conduct than any religious teaching.[14]

Greene reiterates the same view in his essay "The Lost Childhood."

> But in childhood all books are books of divination, telling us about the future, and like the fortune-teller who sees a long journey in the cards or death by water they influence the future.[15]

Greene describes in his essay "The Lost Childhood," the impact of the book *Viper of Milan,* as discussed already. This book, gave him the key subject for all his creations. In the character of the evil personage of Visconti Mastino della Scala, who turned away from a goodness that did not pay to a life of treachery and crime, Greene found the archetype of his anti-heroes. He had been impressed greatly by the character of Quartermain in Rider Haggard's *King Solomon's Mines,* but Quartermain was too good to be true in such an evil world. It was Visconti who confirmed the wickedness of the scenes Greene saw in school and in town. Visconti was an incarnation of Carter, the boy who bullied Greene. Further, it was a reading of Rider Haggard's book and of Prester John that gave Greene that odd African fixation which took him in later life on a reckless trek through Liberia. Similarly, his reading of *Montezuma's Daughter* excited a longing for Mexico—a land he visited in later life and which he loved despite its squalor. Other writers who influenced him were Dixon Brett whose sense of adventure he absorbed and used in his own thrillers or entertainments. The game of poker played on the verge of death in the *Pirate's Aeroplane,* so excited him that he used it in his book, *England Made Me.* The books he read early had a different impact on the shaping of Sartre's character. First, it was reading that provided him with a career. He was moulded to become a writer and to live in the airy realms of ideas. He says:

> I began my life as I shall no doubt end it: among books.[16]

And again,

I found ideas more real than things, because they were the first to give themselves to me and because they gave themselves like things. I met the universe in books: assimilated, classified, labelled and studied, but still impressive; and I confused the chaos of my experiences through books and the hazardous course of real events. Hence my idealism which it took me thirty years to undo.[17]

The last sentence in the passage above suggests that Sartre could finally overthrow his idealism. In Greene's case, however, what books taught him were to be stamped on his consciousness for the rest of life. In the case of Charles Dickens, too, we see the importance of early reading. Dickens was inspired by nursery tales like *Little Red Riding Hood* and the *Arabian Nights*. It was from the latter book that he draws many of his phrases and allusions and also the form of narration. He was to be inspired by Fielding, Smollett, Cervantes and a host of other writers.

And now we must turn to the early awareness of evil that Greene shares with Henry James, Dickens and Sartre. We have already seen how Greene glimpsed Evil first at school in classmates like Crandon and Parlow— "Hell lay about them in their Infancy." Then he was tormented by a boy called Carter who later reincarnated as Visconti, the villain in *The Viper of Milan,* a book he read. "The unfathomable iniquity" of his school which has been described earlier, reaffirmed the presence of Evil forces working in life.

With Henry James, Evil first appeared in the form of the terror of insanity which possessed his father. His father used to see "a damned shape squatting besides him raying out a fetid influence;" his sister, Alice was a prey to suicidal bouts and William James, his brother suffered like his father from the fear of insanity. According to Greene,

> This epileptic idiot, this urge towards death, the damned shape, are a more important background to Henry James' novels than Grosvenor House and late Victorian Society.[18]

Henry James was to describe "the black and merciless things that are behind great possessions" in his book *The Ivory Tower.*

James was to suffer a sense of treachery from relatives who let down the family. His brothers Wilky and Bob were failures drifting from the army to petty business. His cousin Mary Temple Evans was a model in her deadly sickness and her high courage, above all in her hungry grip of life, for the adulterous, wicked women characters like Milly Theale in James' novels. Greene remarks regarding James' study of corruption in *The Wings of the Dove:*

> For to render the highest justice to corruption you must retain your innocence: you have to be conscious all the time within yourself of treachery to something valuable. If Peter Quint is to be rooted in you, so must the child his ghost corrupts.[19]

Sartre's intimations of Evil came from certain incidents that he saw early. His grandfather was bitterly hurt when his publishers tried to exploit him. His early religious inculcation and what he learned from philosophers, moulded his attitude to the world. He writes in his autobiography:

> the world was the prey of Evil; only one salvation: to die to oneself and to the Earth. . . . The clergy took charge of humanity and saved it by the reversibility of merits. . . . Squalid nonsense. I swallowed it down without really understanding it, and I believed it at twenty. . . . I absorbed spites and acerbities which were neither mine nor my grandfather's; the ancient bile of Flaubert, of the Concourts, and of Gautier poisoned me[20]

In the works of Dickens, the taint of the Manichee (Spirit of Evil) is apparent in characters like Fagin, but it is an awareness charged with delight. The evil he saw around him in the form of childhood suffering did not poison him like it did the other writers.

Early in life, too, these writers with their sensitive perception of reality were able to see the inevitability or necessity of death,—an element which so mark their works.

Greene's death-wish emanates from his utter boredom in school-life, his early frustrated love-affair with his brother's governess. His books are pervaded with the idea of death. His anti-heroes long for the final consummation, the deep rest.

With Dickens, the knowledge of death came intuitively. It was suggested to him by one of his earliest toys, a Mask. He writes in *The Christmas Tree:*

> When did that dreadful Mask first look at me? Who put it on, and why was I so frightened that the sight of it is an era in my life?.... Perhaps that fixed and set change coming over a real face infused into my quickened heart some remote suggestion and dread of the universal change that is to come on every face and make it still.[21]

Death is a prominent theme in the works of Dickens. The writer Conrad was a little child at the big Cracow House when his father lay dying. The effect of the scene was to give him that knowledge of death that so marks his works. Greene says about the effect of the scene of death on the future writer's mind.

> It is impossible not to hear in such memories the opening of the door: in some such moment of 'piety, resignation and silence' Conrad's brooding note of sombre dignity and laconic heroism was first struck.[22]

Sartre, like Greene, longed for death early in life to escape the mad terror of living and he finally sublimated the desire and channellized it to a wish to become a writer. Sartre writes in his autobiography:

> I was intoxicated by death because I did not like life: this explains the terror with which it inspires me. Our deepest intentions are an inextricable web of plans and evasions, I can

> see that my mad undertaking to write in order to be forgiven for being alive had, in spite of lies and cowardice, some validity: the proof is that I am still writing, fifty years later.[23]

Sartre's words strongly remind one of what Greene has himself written about his career as a writer:

> I write to escape from boredom.... I sometimes wonder how all those who do not write, compose or paint, can manage to escape the madness, the melancholia and the fear, inherent in the human situation.[24]

Finally, a word may be said about the reaction of Greene and his contemporaries to their schooldays. In the writings of all these writers one common fact stands out: they all loathed their schooldays and wrote against the public school system. We have already seen that Greene's schooldays at Berkhamstead were full of boredom and unhappiness resulting from the injustice and inhibitions of the school system. In his works, his characters loathe school. It is where children are ruined or crippled mentally for life. In *Stambaul Train,* the political exile, Czinner recalls his experiences as a school-master:

> He saw himself for a moment facing a desert of pitch-pine desks, row on row of malicious faces and remembered the times when he had felt round his heart the little cold draughts of disobedience, the secret signals and spurts of disguised laughter threatening his livelihood, for a master who could not keep order must eventually be dismissed.[25]

Mr. Drewitt, the shady lawyer in *Brighton Rock,* shows Pinkie an old school photograph and says:

> A school group, Lancaster College. Not one of the great schools perhaps, but you'll find it in the Public School Year Book . . . a rotten set they were. No esprit de corps.[26]

Both passages bring out the indiscipline that pervaded school in Greene's experience. In fact in his essay "The Last Word" which he contributed to the anthology *The Old School* (he edited this book), he is prompted to erroneously imagine that the public-school system would fast disappear:

> Where then but in this book will the social historians discover a true picture of the vanished system.[27]

His own experience was to make Greene conscious of the educational system in shaping the future of children. In *The Lawless Roads,* he describes the effect of the Communist educational system in Mexico on the future generation:

> Mexican education is fascist or totalitarian whichever you prefer to call it. It is not democratic. . . . It is a little pathetic that muddled idealism which speaks of 'an exact and rational conception of the universe.' One thinks of men like Samuel Butler with hideous crippling childhoods; and in the dry Sonora or Michoacan plains, the homes of Calles and Cardennes, childhood was no doubt crippled—in the Mexican way of the pistol shot and the crooked judge and the cock-fight and the nobody caring for another's life. Who can blame these men if they tried to exercise responsibility.[28]

Greene's contemporary writers too reacted with revulsion to their school-days. George Orwell attended a prep school near Eastbourne, called St. Cyprian's. He was very miserable there and as an adult wrote a long autobiographical essay about his schooldays, "Such, such were the joys." In this, he recreated those early schooldays with detailed loathing.

W.H. Auden is another writer who reacted adversely to school-experience. He writes:

> The best reason I have for opposing fascism is that at school

I lived in a fascist state.[29]

In his essay, "Address for a Prize Day," Auden describes the school as a microcosm of a sick society in need of revolutionary change.

Thus we see that Greene and many writers reacted to early experience negatively. Most of them revolted from the suffering imposed on them by destiny by introducing the theme of revenge in their works. Dickens is the only exception for he took his suffering lightly and was able to throw off the bitterness of the past. What Greene writes about Munro, applies to all the other writers including himself:

> Unhappiness wonderfully aids the memory, and, the best stories of Munro are all of childhood, its humour and its anarchy as well as its cruelty and unhappiness.[30]

NOTES

1. Greene, Graham, "The Burden of Childhood" in *Collected Essays*, The Bodley Head, London, 1969, p. 127.
2. Quennell, Peter, *The Sign of the Fish,* Collins, London, 1960, pp. 61-62.
3. Greene, Graham, "The Burden of Childhood," p. 127.
4. Wilson, Angus, *The World of Charles Dickens,* Secker and Warburg, London, 1970, pp. 51-52.
5. Greene, Graham, "The Burden of Childhood," p. 128.
6. Ibid., p. 127.
7. Ibid.
8. Wilson, Angus, *The World of Charles Dickens,* p. 57.
9. Ibid., p. 58.
10. Kipling, Rudyard, "Baa Baa Black Sheep" as quoted by Graham Greene in "The Burden of Childhood" p. 128.
11. Sartre, Jean-Paul, *Words,* Penguin in Association with

Hamish Hamilton, London, 1972, pp. 14-15.

12. Greene, Graham, *A Gun for Sale*, Heinemann, London, 1959.
13. Sartre, Jean-Paul, *Words*, p. 170.
14. Greene, Graham, *A Sort of Life*, Penguin, London, 1971, p. 40.
15. Greene, Graham, "The Lost Childhood," p. 13.
16. Sartre, Jean-Paul, *Words*, p. 29.
17. Ibid., p. 34.
18. Greene, Graham, *Collected Essays*, p. 31.
19. Ibid., p. 28.
20. Sartre, Jean-Paul: *Words*, pp. 112-13.
21. Dickens, Charles, "The Christmas Tree" as quoted in Angus Wilson's *The World of Charles Dickens*, p. 9.
22. Greene, Graham, "Henry James, the Private Universe" in *Collected Essays*, p. 34.
23. Sartre, Jean-Paul, *Words*, p. 121.
24. Greene, Graham, *Ways of Escape*, Bodley Head, London, 1980, p. 174.
25. Greene, Graham, *Stamboul Train*, Heinemann, London, 1959, p. 65.
26. Greene, Graham, *Brighton Rock*, Heinemann, London, 1955, p. 52.
27. Bergonzi, Bernard, "Men Among Boys and Boys Among Men," in *Reading the Thirties*, Macmillan, London, 1979, p. 29.
28. Greene, Graham, *The Lawless Roads*, Heinemann, London, 1955, p. 84.
29. Auden, W.H., *The Old School*, ed. Graham Greene, Cape, London, 1934, p. 45.
30. Greene, Graham, "The Burden of Childhood," pp. 128-29.

Conclusion: Return to Childhood: Pendele

The method of psychoanalysis is to bring the patient back to the idea which he is repressing; a long journey backwards without maps, catching a clue here and a clue there . . . until one has to face the general idea, the pain or the memory.[1]

"The general idea, the pain or the memory" Greene has often referred to in his works is the racial childhood of man, that state of innocence, primordial and pristine that modern man has lost in this mad scramble called civilisation. According to Greene, man has only one hope of survival left—he must return to childhood and relive its myths. He must be shorn of all the sophisticated accretions, the violence, the evil, the cunning that represents civilisation. In preceding chapters of this thesis, I have already discussed man's "Judas complex" or his going astray from a healthy life owing to a lost childhood; I have also discussed man's original sin in the form of sex which made him an outcaste from the Garden of Eden or bliss; we have studied the great aboriginal calamity that seems to have overtaken man, the failure that hovers over man's life and the doom inherent in all human ventures; we have seen the hell called Greeneland, that is our world—one stretch of crime and squalor. Greene's belief is that we must save mankind from a holocaust by returning to that state of life, where the artifices of civilisation have not disguised our true, pure emotions.

Querry, a successful architect, in *A Burnt-Out Case* undertakes the journey back to childhood when he goes to Africa and stumbles upon Pendele—a state of dancing, singing, and unalloyed joy which brings to him the peace he could not find in the portals of western civilisation. And, I believe, Querry is none other than Greene himself, the successful man of letters who much earlier than his character, Querry, undertook a perilous journey to Liberia, to the heart of the Dark Continent. Here he had the transient vision of happiness,

> the sensation of having come home, for here one was finding associations with a personal and racial childhood, one was being scared by the same old witches.[2]

Greene's language shows a psychoanalytical mind at work as he tries to retrace the path of mankind back to the point where the racial childhood was left behind. Marlowe's trip to the Heart of Darkness led him to a horror of primitive barbarism, but Greene's journey without maps,

> reinforced a sense of disappointment with what man had made out of the primitive, what he had made out of childhood.[3]

According to Greene, psychology has discovered and reinforced the necessity and yearning of some people of today to return to a state where things were still in a pristine childhood. Thus, the discoveries of Freud and the perilous journeys of explorers of the Dark Continent like Mungo Park, Livingstone, Rimbaud, Conrad and Greene himself are just two different methods of going back to one's origins. Greene says in *Journey Without Maps:*

> 'The heart of darkness' was common to us both. Freud has made us conscious as we have never been before of those ancestral threads which still exist in our unconscious minds to lead us back.[4]

The childhood of civilisation has been ravished by an adult, so-called progressive modernisation. In Africa, Greene realised that the civilisation he had left behind in the West had exchanged "the sense of supernatural evil" for "the small human viciousness." The Eden of Childhood had been invaded by the adult world, "the sinless, graceless, chromium world." Meaninglessness and boredom have overcome mankind's senses. One must go to "Africa"—a state of innocence, signifying recapture of the creative sensitivity to a supernatural power. This power denoted the synthesis of good and evil that has been lost in our civilisation. Writing about the bush-devils of Liberia, Greene says that the significance of their supernatural authority cannot be comprehended in a theological system of our civilised rationality:

> In a Christian land we have grown so accustomed to the idea of a spiritual war, of God and Satan, that this supernatural world, which is neither good nor evil but simply Power, is almost beyond sympathetic comprehension. Not quite: for those witches which haunted our childhood were neither good nor evil. They terrified us with their power, but we knew all the time that we must not escape them. They simply demanded recognition: flight was a weakness.[5]

In childhood, Greene was precociously aware of supernatural forces behind experience. In an autobiographical passage in *Journey Without Maps*, he tells us how in childhood, he was haunted in sleep by the fear of "something outside that has got to come in." Later, the unseen presence was personified by the Princess of Time, the poisoned flowers, an old Arab, Tibetan Warriors, and the inevitable witch at the corner cupboard. Greene tells us:

> You couldn't call these things evil, as Peter Quint in 'The Turn of the Screw' was evil, with his carroty hair and his white face of damnation. That story of James belongs to the Christian, the orthodox imagination. Mine were devils only in the African sense of beings who controlled power.[6]

Greene says that the "odd African fixation" or love for the Dark Continent came to him in childhood itself when he read Rider

Haggard's *King Solomon's Mines*. The adventurous tales of Allain Quartermain and Sir Henry Curtis made them his earliest heroes and the ancient Gagool possessed his imagination:

> Gagool I could recognise—didn't she wait for me in dreams every night in the passage by the linen cupboard, near the nursery door? and she continues to wait, when the mind is sick or tired, though now she is dressed in the theological garments of despair.[7]

Gagool was a power of the same species as the supernatural powers in Africa, neither good nor evil which Greene encountered among the bush-devils.

In his book, *Journey Without Maps*, Greene records the external filth, disease, cruelty, hardship and squalid discomfort he came across in Africa, but his subconscious mind is occupied in "psychoanalytic prospecting with a view to locating himself in his spiritual home, the heart of darkness."[8] He evolves the idea of Africa, as the actual heart of mankind, where his earliest longings lie buried. He writes in *In Search of a Character:*

> Africa will always be the Africa of the Victorian Atlas, the blank unexplored continent, the shape of the human heart.[9]

In Liberia, Greene was able to realize why there had been that struggle in his childhood between transitory moments of happiness and utter meaningless and boredom. In childhood, on the one hand he had inklings of being closer to his origins: on the other hand, the adult world drew him away from that state. The struggle had been between:

> the sense that one was nearer than one had ever been to the racial source, to satisfying the desire for an instinctive way of life, the sense of release . . . counterbalanced by the boredom of childhood too, that agonising boredom of 'apartness' which came before one had learnt the fatal trick of transferring

emotion.[10]

So, the message of Greene's work is that the childhood of mankind is lost. This is the major cause of all the wars and dissensions, loneliness and unhappiness of modern man. One must regain it, if one is to have an emotionally ripe, spiritually meaningful existence. Greene first became aware of the necessity for such a rejuvenation of life when he discovered in Africa "a thing I had never possessed: a love for life."[11]

Greene was very sick and lying in Zigi's town, almost dead. It was then that it dawned on him that he had never really loved life. Africa, the heart of racial man, the key to the secrets of childhood, opened up a vista of existence, that proved as strong as a religious conversion:

> I had always assumed before, as a matter of course, that death was desirable. It seemed that night an important discovery. It was like a conversion, and I had never experienced a conversion before (I had not been converted to a religious faith. I had been convinced in the probability of its creed).[12]

Here, in Africa, he found

> the sense of pleasure keener, the sense of terror deeper and purer.[13]

In Africa, Greene often felt that time was suspended. The mad hurry of civilisation had been left behind in Europe. As he trekked through the heart of the Dark Continent he felt an urge to laugh and felt free of restraints.

He laments the loss of this childhood keenness to enjoy simple pleasures. Our senses are overlaid with the superficial gloss of civilisation:

> It isn't a gain to have turned the witch or the masked secret dancer, the sense of supernatural evil, into the small human

viciousness of the thin distinguished military grey head in Kensington Gardens with the soft lips and the eyes which dwelt with dull lustre on girls and boys of a certain age.[14]

His lament for this loss of man's innocence reminds one of William Wordsworth who in his "Ode on Intimations of Immortality from Recollections of Early Childhood" sorrows for the passing away of the pure, deep perceptions of a child.

There was a time when meadow, grove and stream,
The earth, and every common sight,
To me did seem
Apparell'd in celestial light,
The glory and the freshness of a dream.
It is not now as it hath been of yore;
Turn wheresoe'er I may,
  By night or day,
The things which I have seen
  I now can see no more.[15]

Greene's *Journey Without Maps* was first published in 1936. *A Burnt-Out Case* came out in 1961, a duration of twenty-five years from the *Journey Without Maps*. In *A Burnt-Out Case*, Greene harps again on the theme of retracing our steps back to our racial childhood. Querry, the hero of this novel, is an architect, to whom worldly success and renown have come unreservedly. However, he is overcome by a sense of the futility of all his fame and success. All his grand achievements, he realizes, were out of love for himself. His heart had remained devoid of compassion and it was an arid desert in which there was no love, no laughter. He comes to Africa in just such a state of spiritual vacuity. He is *A Burnt-Out Case*, a spiritual leper in whom the disease has run its full course. He represents the same adult civilisation, "the graceless chromium world" described by Greene in *The Lawless Roads*. Here in Africa he stumbles on "Pendele," a childhood myth, a world of spontaneous "singing and dancing and games and prayers." The word

"Pendele" is uttered by his servant Deo Gratias in the darkness where Querry is caught in a shallow marsh. Deo Gratias' adult memory has only dimly retained the semblance of the Eden of childhood. Here, at last, Querry feels he has come to peace. He talks to the superior about this. The superior's reaction is:

> People have to grow up. We are called to more complicated things than that.[16]

Querry's reply to the Superior, is certainly Greene's own answer to the problem of human unhappiness. He says:

> there's also something about having to be as little children if we are to inherit. . . . We've grown up rather badly. The complications have become too complex. . . . If your god wanted an adult world he should have given us an adult brain.[17]

Here Greene implies the responsibility of God for the loss of innocence and unhappiness. As the unintelligible chant of the Africans comes to his ears, Querry is reminded in a subtle subconscious way of ancestral voices. The faint memories of childhood tug at the mind and he feels at peace in a sort of psychological regression to a state without thought or belief.

In *A Burnt-Out Case*, Greene, through Querry was not to realize his cherished desire to regain childhood innocence and happiness. Querry is stalked by the world he has left behind. Parkinson, a journalist wants to make a good write-up for his paper by creating a saint out of Querry's suffering and his redemption through "Pendele." Besides this, Mary Rycker proves a femme fatale and moves Querry's heart with pity by her poor plight. He is killed by Mary's husband who becomes suspicious of Querry's interest in her.

However, Greene was to realize his aim of regaining childhood bliss in his book *Travels with my Aunt,* published in 1969, eight years after Querry missed Pendele. In *Travel's with my Aunt,*

Greene identifies his ambitions with the character, Henry Pulling. Pulling is at first, a man of dull, phlegmatic disposition, whose job of a bank clerk has conditioned him into a stagnant existence restricted to cultivating dahlias and the major next door. His life is one long, monotonous existence of inactive goodness. Aunt Augusta suddenly appears on the scene like a fairy and makes him aware of the necessity of returning to the keener pleasures of childhood if he wanted to escape his dreary existence, (which in Greenesque terms represents again our dull unhappy adult world of rationalized norms). Pulling visits with Aunt Augusta (playing Sancho Panza to her), all the shady haunts of the world where Aunt Augusta introduces him to crime. He becomes involved in a smuggling gang in Paraguay. In this way, he regains the exciting childhood sensations which once caused his heart to jump at burglars and Indian thugs and fires and Jack the Ripper.

In this book, *Travels with my Aunt,* Greene has looked at the idea of returning to a childhood state in a more comic vein. The activities of Henry Pulling and Aunt Augusta are unreal and picaresque and smack of debauchery and crime, but Greene was trying to make a point which he could not successfully conclude in *Journey Without Maps* and *A Burnt-Out Case.*

In his novel *The Human Factor,* Greene indulges his nostalgia to return to his childhood in the character of Castle. The place names are not changed in this novel. Castle's birthplace is, like Greene's, Berkhamstead. For example:

> Castle was usually able to catch the six thirty-five train from Euston. This brought him to Berkhamstead punctually at seven twelve. . . . In a bizarre profession anything which belongs to an everyday routine gains great value—perhaps that was one reason why, when he came back from South Africa, he chose to return to his birth place.[18]

Castle echoes the same idea when he tells his wife regarding Sam, his son:

> I'd like Sam to stay put in one place so that when he goes away he'll be able to come back. To something he knew in childhood like you came back. To something old.[19]

And now, we must see the implications of Greene's views on childhood as studied in the preceding chapters. Childhood, in the sense of the happiness of children in general, and in the meaning of innocence in the adult must be preserved by mankind, by humanitarian bodies of the world if peace and happiness is to be restored to our earth. The Pinkies, Ravens, Anthonys, Mintys, Corals, Brigittas—and the whole retinue of Greenesque characters can be saved from being mutilated spiritually, if conscientious human beings and responsible adults arrange a better life for them, if society gives them a better deal, if organisations like the Unicef do their best to make the childhood of millions happy. Parents must educate themselves to understand the psychology of their children so that they might not wreck lives like Anthonys and Andrews by misdirected parental interference. Educational systems must be reorganized so that children like Anthony, Andrews, and Minty may not go adrift, carrying the wound of schooldays in their hearts. Governments must remove the poverty of slums where Pinkie and his like are born and who drift into a realm of miserable violence. Books, healthy and life-inspiring must be made available to children when they begin to decode secrets of the written letter, so that the wrong influences are not wrought on them.

Ronald Russell very aptly sums up the relation between a child's early upbringing and his reactions in later life. I think Greene would whole-heartedly recommend this poem to parents because it endorses his own views:

> A child that lives with ridicule
> learns to be timid.
> A child that lives with criticism
> learns to condemn.
> A child that lives with distrust
> learns to be deceitful.

A child that lives with antagonism
  learns to be hostile.
A child that lives with affection
  learns to love.
A child that lives with truth
  learns justice.
A child that lives with praise
  learns to appreciate.
A child that lives with sharing
  learns to be considerate.
A child that lives with knowledge
  learns wisdom.
A child that lives with patience
  learns to be tolerant.
A child that lives with happiness
  will find love and beauty.[20]

Greene writes in *Journey Without Maps* that only by a return to its origins can civilization be saved:

> There are others, of course, who prefer to look a stage ahead, for whom Intourist provides cheap tickets, into a plausible future, but my journey represented a distrust of any future based on what we are.[21]

Henry Vaughan poetizes the same emotion in the poem "The Retreat":

Happy those early days! When I
Shined in my angel infancy.
Before I understood this place
Appointed for my second race, . . .
O, how I long to travel back,
And tread again that ancient track!
Some men a forward motion love,
But I by backward steps would move,

And when this dust falls to the urn,
In that state I came, return.[22]

Maria Montessori has written that the key to the understanding of the adult, of the human race, in general, of its follies and grandeur, lies in the understanding of the child. It is in this complete sense, that the "Child is the Father of Man" as Wordsworth said. Montesorri writes:

> The Swedish poet and author Ellen Key prophesied that our century would be the century of the child. . . . No one could have foreseen then that the child held within himself a secret of life, able to lift the veil from the mysteries of the human soul; that he represented an unknown quantity, the discovery of which might enable the adult to solve his individual and social problems. This aspect may prove the foundations of a new science of child study, capable of influencing the whole social life of man.[23]

To understand Graham Greene's works in all its totality and to be able to discover in his life and attitudes a meaningful pattern in which subsidiary themes co-ordinate into a composite whole, one must approach his mind from this point in time (when he lives and writes) and to retrogress to the first building blocks of experience in childhood. Gradually, like sudden revelations, one begins to see a connection between his most varied themes. It is like becoming aware after a passage of time, of the meaning of God's inscrutable plans. What importance does Greene's misery, boredom and suicidal attempts at school have when we consider his creative output? Can we not link these with his desire to regain a joy in living by risking its total loss—an experiment he tried out in his dangerous Liberian trek? And is this risk not related to his idea of damnation as a risk which is necessary to gain spiritual salvation—an idea postulated in *The Power and the Glory* and *The Heart of the Matter* ?

We discern a network of interrelated themes in his novels. The centre of this network is his childhood. From here one may see emanating the labyrinthine ways of Graham Greene. In fact, life is like a child's jigsaw map which is as yet unassembled. Only as one goes on living does the map take shape. This is the idea contained in Greene's quotation of Oliver Wendell Holmes at the beginning of *Journey Without Maps:*

> The life of an individual is in many ways like a child's dissected map. If I could live a hundred years, keeping my intelligence to the last, I feel as if I could put the pieces together until they made a properly connected whole. . . . If I could go back on the whole, as we look at the child's map when it is put together, I feel that I should have my whole life intelligently laid out before me.[24]

Is the map of Greene's life complete? Not yet. Greene is 85 now. He grows older in body, but his continual creative output testifies to a mind that returns again and again to the embryonic stage of life—childhood. It is a confession about himself as he quotes Gustave Herbert at the beginning of his novel, *Ways of Escape:*

> As my body continues on its journey, my thoughts keep turning back and bury themselves in days past.[25]

So strong is this nostalgia to return to one's origins that with an irony characteristic of his statements, he prophesies that his end lies in his beginning. He begins his autobiography with the words which I feel are a fitting finale to this study:

> If I had known it, the whole future must have lain all the time along those Berkhamstead streets. . . . Everything one was to become must have been there, for better or worse. One's future might have been prophesied from the shape of the houses as from the lines of the hand;. . . . Here in Berkhamstead was the first mould of which the shape was to be endlessly reproduced . . . and I feel it would be strange if,

through the unconscious sources of action, through folly or wisdom, I were not brought back to die there in the place where everything was born.[26]

NOTES

1. Greene, Graham, *Journey Without Maps*, Heinemann, London, 1950, pp. 109-10.
2. Ibid., p. 104.
3. Ibid., p. 278.
4. Ibid., pp. 251-52.
5. Ibid., p. 10.
6. Ibid., p. 213.
7. Ibid., p. 219.
8. Ibid., p. 15.
9. Greene, Graham, *In Search of a Character:* Two African Journals, Bodley Head, London, 1961, p. 123.
10. Greene, Graham, *Journey Without Maps*, p. 193.
11. Ibid., p. 206.
12. Ibid., p. 278.
13. Ibid.
14. Ibid.
15. Wordsworth, William, "Ode on Intimations of Immortality from Recollections of Early Childhood," *The Golden Treasury* Bk. IV, ed. Francis Turner Palgrave, Oxford Univ. Press, London, 1959, pp. 136-37.
16. Greene, Graham, *A Burnt-Out Case*. The Reprint Society, London, 1962, pp. 87-88.
17. Ibid., p. 88.
18. Greene, Graham, *The Human Factor,* The Bodley Head, London, 1980, p. 19.
19. Ibid., p. 106.
20. Russell, Ronald, "Lessons from Life" in *Better Life*, Sept. 1981, p. 1.

21. Greene, Graham, A *Journey Without Maps*, p. 16.
22. Vaughan, Henry, "The Retreat," in *The Oxford Book of English Verse* (1250-1900) ed. Arthur Quiller Couch, Clarendon, 1931, p. 295.
23. Montessori, Maris, *The Secret of Childhood,* Orient Longman, Bombay, 1978, pp. 3-4.
24. Wendell Holmes, Oliver, Quoted by Graham Greene in *Journey Without Maps*, p. 2.
25. Herbert Gustavc, as quoted in Graham Greene's *Ways of Escape*, The Bodley Head, London, 1980, p. 7.
26. Greene, Graham, *A Sort of Life,* Penguin, London, 1971, pp. 11-12.